# FROM VISION
# TO DIVINE PROVISION

## *The Islamic Art of Sacred Manifestation*

# FATIMAH
## LINDA HOWARD

First Edition, 2025
Publisher: Alturnative, LLC

Paperback ISBN # 978-0-9910143-5-4
Hardback ISBN # 978-0-9910143-6-1
eBook ISBN # 978-0-9910143-7-8

Connect with Linda (Fatimah) Howard for Speaking, Workshops, and Retreat Facilitation. Author of *Crescent Over Crossroads* and Islamic personal development consultant, she brings the principles of Islamic manifestation to your mosque, retreat, or personal development gathering through inspiring presentations and interactive workshops.

For speaking inquiries and program details,
visit www.withlindahoward.com
or email engage@withlindahoward.com.

In the name of Allah,
the Most Gracious,
the Most Merciful.

# DEDICATION

This book is dedicated to the cherished memory of my mother, Gertrude Howard Saunders. Allah blessed the earth with her presence for 101 years.

She was my first teacher in faith and forgiveness, my fiercest protector, and the most constant example of what it means to trust God with grace and quiet strength.

Her belief in me never wavered. Her prayers, encouragement and example shaped the woman I am today. This book is a reflection of the faith she lived so effortlessly and the legacy she left in every soul she touched.

May Allah reward you abundantly and grant you Jannat al-Firdaus.

# THANK YOU
### *All Praise and Thanks to Allah*

First and always, I thank Allah—the Source of all provision, inspiration, and mercy.

> *"And He giveth you of all that ye ask for. But if ye count the favours of Allah, never will ye be able to number them."*
> (Qur'an 14:34)

Ya Allah, writing this book has brought me closer to You. Thank You for the inspiration, the clarity, and the strength. Every word in this book that brings another soul closer to You is from You. Any shortcomings are my own.

### *To My Family, With Love*

To my parents, Gertrude and Isaac "Ike" Howard, Jr.—thank you for grounding me in love, faith, and purpose.

To my departed siblings—your influence and presence are never far from my heart.

To my extended family—my nieces and nephews—thank you for being there for me and for each other.

A special thank you to my only living sibling, my big sister Brenda Ruffin. Your daily encouragement, unwavering belief in me, and consistent thirst for knowledge lift my spirit and fuel my passion. Your words echo in my heart and help carry this book into being.

### *To the Sisters' Steadfast Saturdays Circle*

Thank you for believing in the vision of Sisters' Steadfast Saturdays—enough to show up, even when it meant driving over an hour to my home.

It was through your presence, your honesty, and the sacred conversations we shared that this book came to life.

You inspired me to put into words my process for sacred manifestation.

# CONTENTS

PART THREE

# APPENDIX

# HOW TO USE THIS BOOK

## FOR MUSLIM READERS

This book serves as both a spiritual guide and a practical workbook. While you may be familiar with many of the Islamic concepts, Part I establishes the crucial foundation that makes this framework authentically Islamic rather than simply positive thinking with Islamic language. Even if you're well-versed in Islamic teachings, this foundation section will deepen your understanding of how traditional concepts like *du'a* (supplication), *tawakkul* (trust and reliance on Allah), and *shukr* (gratitude) work together in manifestation.

Why the foundation matters: Many well-meaning approaches to Islamic personal development inadvertently borrow from secular manifestation without proper Islamic grounding. Part I ensures your practice remains centered on *Tawheed* (Oneness of Allah) and prophetic guidance.

You'll find Arabic terms throughout, explained at first use in each chapter. The Glossary provides pronunciations and detailed explanations to support your learning.

Each chapter includes Journey Prompts and du'as to deepen your practice and help you apply these principles in your unique circumstances.

## FOR NON-MUSLIM READERS

While this book is written from an Islamic perspective, readers of other monotheistic faiths will find universal principles of prayer, intention, and divine trust. Many concepts supported by Qur'anic references align with verses in the Bible and Torah.

To help you navigate:

- Arabic terms are explained at first use in each chapter, with comprehensive definitions in the Glossary
- The word "Allah" is the Arabic term for God. While used by Arabic-speaking Christians and Jews, for Muslims it specifically refers to the One Divine Creator who has no partners and possesses the 99 Beautiful Names (listed in the Appendix) such as *Ar-Rahman* (The Most Merciful) and *Ar-Razzaq* (The Provider)
- Du'a means supplication—direct, personal prayer to Allah
- The framework emphasizes surrendering to divine will rather than trying to control outcomes

## GETTING THE MOST FROM THIS BOOK

**Before You Begin**

- Set an intention (*niyyah*) for why you're reading this
- Keep a journal nearby for Journey Prompts and reflection exercises
- Approach with an open heart, ready for spiritual transformation

**As You Read**

- Don't rush—this is a transformative journey that requires reflection
- Complete the Journey Prompts—they're designed to help you apply concepts personally
- Allow integration time between chapters to practice what you've learned
- Trust the process—some insights will unfold gradually through practice

**Key Features to Notice**

- Spiritual Takeaways—summarize each chapter's core message
- Du'as—supplications you can incorporate into daily practice
- Real Stories—personal examples of these principles in action

- Journey Prompts—reflection questions for deeper application

## USING THE APPENDIX

Your appendix serves as a comprehensive reference guide:

- The 99 Beautiful Names—Allah's attributes for contemplation and du'a
- Glossary—Arabic terms with pronunciation guides and clear definitions
- Complete Citations—All Qur'anic verses and Hadith references for further study
- Qur'anic Affirmations—Verses adapted for personal reflection
- Du'a Collection—All supplications from the book, plus additional du'as for daily use

This resource section transforms the book into a practical manual you'll return to throughout your spiritual journey.

## SUGGESTED READING APPROACHES

Complete Journey (Recommended)—Read straight through, completing exercises as you go. This provides the most comprehensive and transformative experience.

Reference Style—Use specific chapters and appendix sections for particular situations or spiritual practices.

Study Group—Work through Journey Prompts with others, discussing and sharing experiences for collective growth.

## CREATING YOUR PRACTICE SPACE

Consider preparing:

- A quiet space for reflection and du'a
- A dedicated journal for this spiritual work
- Regular times for daily practices (Chapter 12)
- Materials for your vision board (Chapter 13)

## A Note on Arabic Terms

Don't feel overwhelmed by Arabic terminology. These words carry spiritual significance that English translations cannot fully capture. The book introduces each term clearly, and the glossary provides pronunciation guides. Embrace them gradually—they will enrich your understanding and connection to this practice.

Remember: This book is not just about reading—it's about becoming. Let it change you from the inside out.

> *"Allah does not change a people's lot unless they change what is in their hearts."*
> (Qur'an 13:11)

## Journey Prompts

1. What draws you to this book at this moment in your life? What are you hoping to transform?
2. Which area of your life most needs divine alignment right now— career, relationships, health, or spiritual growth?
3. Write a letter to yourself describing who you hope to become through this journey. Include both worldly and spiritual aspirations.

# INTRODUCTION
## THE DIVINE LAW OF ATTRACTION

In recent years, books and courses on the Law of Attraction have inspired millions to believe in the power of intention. While these teachings offer valuable insights, they often overlook a fundamental truth central to Islamic belief: There is no power or might except by the will of Allah (*La hawla wa la quwwata illa billah*).

The traditional Law of Attraction teaches that we attract into our lives whatever we focus on—whether consciously or subconsciously. It suggests that our thoughts, feelings, and energy emit a frequency that draws similar experiences into our reality. However, for Muslims and those seeking a more spiritually grounded approach, this framework is incomplete.

The idea of "manifesting" has captured the imagination of many. Books like The Secret and The Magic speak of gratitude as a magnetic force—drawing abundance the way metal is drawn to a magnet. While the language may differ, the heart of this concept is not new to us as Muslims.

Yes, gratitude multiplies blessings. Yes, clear intention shapes our reality. But New Age messaging around gratitude attributes this power to an impersonal universe rather than recognizing its true source: Allah, *Ar-Razzaq* (The Provider), *Al-Karim* (The Most Generous).

As Muslims, we've always known what others are just discovering. Long before "manifestation" became a buzzword, we understood the link between gratitude and abundance:

> *"And remember! your Lord caused to be declared*
> *(publicly):*
> *'If ye are grateful, I will add more (favours) unto you ....'"*
> (Qur'an 14:7)

Believing that gratitude multiplies blessings isn't just positive thinking—it's divine promise. When we show *shukr* (gratitude), we don't attract abundance through cosmic magnetism; we open our hearts to receive from the One who owns all treasures. When we make du'a with conviction, we're not sending wishes into a void; we're conversing with the One who says "Be," and it is.

This book offers a unique perspective: an Islamic reframing of manifestation and intentional living. We'll explore how these concepts align with Islamic principles, creating a powerful synthesis of faith and personal development that honors both your worldly aspirations and your eternal purpose.

Allah tells us in the Qur'an:

---

*"And for those who fear Allah, He (ever) prepares a way out, And He provides for him from (sources) he never could imagine."*
(Qur'an 65:2-3)

---

This verse reminds us that it is Allah, Ar-Razzaq, who is the true source of all provision and blessings. Our role is to align our hearts, intentions, and actions with His divine will, recognizing that every blessing—including our ability to dream and strive—comes from Him alone.

The difference is profound. Where secular manifestation attributes power to an impersonal universe, Islam recognizes Allah as the conscious, merciful Source of all that exists. Where others speak of cosmic energy, we understand divine decree. Where they teach self-empowerment, we learn God-consciousness.

I need to be honest with you—this book is as much for me as it is for you. Every page I've written has been a reminder to myself first. We are, by nature, forgetful beings living in a world of endless distractions. We need constant reminders of what it means to dream with faith, to desire with devotion, and to pursue our goals while keeping our hearts anchored in the Divine.

If you've ever felt torn between your worldly dreams and your spiritual aspirations...

If you've made du'a for more—more peace, more purpose, more provision—and wondered if wanting "more" makes you less grateful...

If you've been curious about manifestation but uncomfortable with its secular packaging...

This book is for you.

Not because I have all the answers, but because together, we can explore a framework that honors both your dreams and your *deen* (religion). A framework that teaches you to visualize with faith, plan with prayer, and pursue your aspirations knowing that:

There is no power and no might except with Allah. (*La hawla wa la quwwata illa billah*)

Welcome to a journey of sacred manifestation—where your biggest dreams meet your deepest faith.

## SEVEN STEPS INSPIRED BY ISLAMIC TEACHINGS

The journey from desire to divine fulfillment isn't random—it follows a sacred pattern that Muslims have practiced for centuries. While contemporary manifestation culture speaks of "raising your vibration" or "aligning with the universe," Islam offers something far more profound: a complete framework for aligning your will with the Divine Will.

The seven steps that follow aren't new inventions. They're timeless Islamic principles, now organized to help you navigate from intention to fulfillment with Allah at the center of every stage. Each step builds upon the last, creating a spiritual progression that honors both your worldly aspirations and your eternal purpose.

## Here's how the journey unfolds:

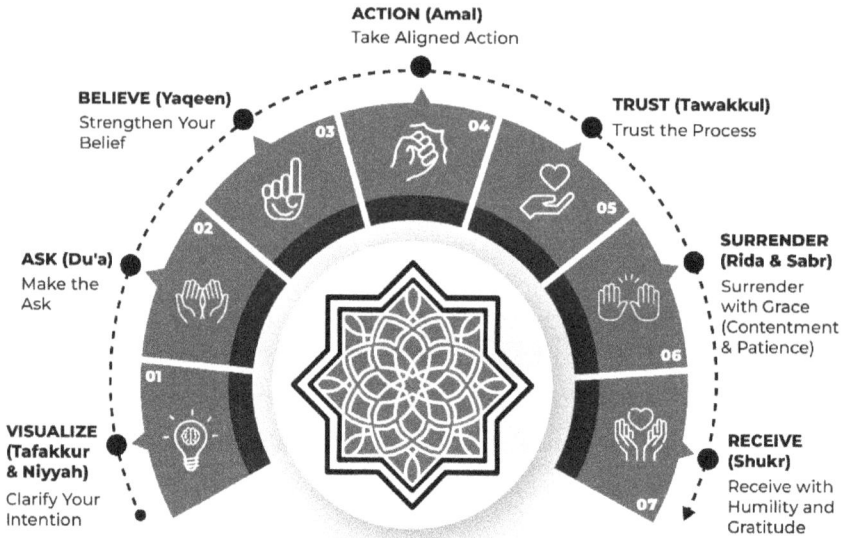

The table below explains these principles in more detail.

## THE SEVEN-STEP SACRED MANIFESTATION FRAMEWORK

| Focus Area | Islamic-Centered Term | Explanation |
|---|---|---|
| Visualize - Clarify Your Intention | Tafakkur (Contemplation) & Niyyah (Intention) | Before asking, reflect with sincerity. Visualization helps clarify what you seek and why—aligning your desires with your values and the pleasure of Allah. |
| Ask - Make the Ask | Du'a (Supplication) | You ask from the only One who can provide—Allah. You speak your need clearly and trust His Mercy and Wisdom. |
| Believe - Strengthen Your Belief | Yaqeen (Certainty in Allah) | Believe not in the universe's randomness but in Allah's mercy, might, and responsiveness to sincere prayer. |

| Focus Area | Islamic-Centered Term | Explanation |
|---|---|---|
| Action - Take Aligned Action | Amal (Acting in Divine Alignment) | Work diligently toward your goal. Break it into smaller, actionable steps and consistently put in the effort. *"Tie your camel and then put your trust in Allah."* (*Jami' at-Tirmidhi*, Book of Zuhd, Hadith 2517) |
| Trust - Trust the Process | Tawakkul (Trust and Reliance on Allah) | You put in the effort and leave the outcome to Allah. You trust His timing, even when it differs from yours. |
| Surrender - Surrender with Grace | Rida (Contentment) & Sabr (Patience) | Release your need to control how or when Allah answers your du'a. Surrender to His will with trust and serenity. |
| Receive - Receive with Humility | Shukr (Gratitude) | When the blessing comes—big or small—you receive it with humility and gratitude, acknowledging it as from Allah alone. |

## WHAT THIS BOOK WILL OFFER YOU

This book is both a guide and a companion on your journey toward intentional, faith-centered living.

Part I lays the foundation, offering a clear understanding of essential Islamic concepts and terms related to manifestation, intention, and divine alignment.

Part II walks you through a spiritually grounded, seven-step framework.

- Visualize through *Tafakkur* (Contemplation) and set your *Niyyah* (Intention)
- Ask with sincerity through *Du'a* (Supplication)
- Believe with unwavering *Yaqeen* (Certainty)
- Act with purpose

- Trust in divine timing with *Tawakkul* (Trust and reliance on Allah) (Reliance on Allah)
- Surrender with grace through *Riḍā* (Contentment) and *Ṣabr* (Patience)
- Receive with heartfelt *Shukr* (Gratitude)

Part III offers practical tools and exercises to help you move from vision to application. You'll find guided journey prompts, Qur'anic reflections, and faith-based practices to deepen your understanding and integrate these principles into your life. Together, we'll explore how to:

- Overcome limiting beliefs
- Reframe internal narratives
- Build a sacred du'a practice
- Strengthen your connection to Allah, the Source of all provision and mercy

Whether you're a Muslim seeking to align your personal growth with your faith or someone exploring an Islamic lens on manifestation and purposeful living, this book offers a unique path to transformation, rooted in divine remembrance, trust, and surrender.

As we begin this sacred journey, let us reflect on the words of the Prophet Muhammad (PBUH):

---

*"Allah says: 'I am as My servant thinks I am. I am with him when he remembers Me. If he remembers Me to himself, I remember him to Myself; and if he remembers Me in an*

---

### Understanding Hadith

Hadith are recorded sayings, actions, and approvals of Prophet Muhammad (PBUH). They serve as the second source of Islamic guidance after the Qur'an, helping Muslims understand how to apply Qur'anic principles in daily life. This book primarily uses hadith from the most authentic collections (Sahih al-Bukhari, Sahih Muslim, etc.) that have been verified by Islamic scholars for accuracy and reliability.

When you see a hadith citation, you're reading words or examples directly from the Prophet (PBUH) who Muslims believe received divine guidance.

*assembly, I remember him in an assembly better than it..."'*
(*Sahih al-Bukhari, Book of Tawhid*, Hadith 7405,
Also in: *Sahih Muslim*, Book of Dhikr, Hadith 2675)

This journey is the place where dreams meet du'a, du'a fuels direction, and direction unfolds into divine destiny.

Let us begin with open hearts, ready to unlock the divine potential within us and all around us.

## JOURNEY PROMPTS

1. How have you viewed manifestation before reading this introduction? What excites or concerns you about an Islamic approach?
2. What dreams have you been hesitant to make du'a for, thinking they might be "too worldly"?
3. Write about a time when Allah gave you something better than what you asked for. How did this experience shape your trust in divine wisdom?
4. This week, begin each morning by thanking Allah for three specific blessings before making any requests and set aside a specific time each day for reading and reflection. Choose a quiet space that will become your sacred study area.

# PART ONE
## FOUNDATION

*"On no soul doth Allah Place a burden greater than it can bear. It gets every good that it earns, and it suffers every ill that it earns. "*
(Qur'an 2:286)

"Thee do we worship,
and Thine aid we seek."
(Qur'an 1:5)

# CHAPTER ONE
## ALLAH IS THE ONLY SOURCE: WHAT ISLAMIC MANIFESTATION REALLY MEANS

### RECLAIMING MANIFESTATION FOR MUSLIMS

The word "manifestation" might feel foreign to your Islamic vocabulary, but the principles it describes are deeply familiar. Long before vision boards and affirmations became popular, Muslims understood the profound connection between gratitude, intention, and divine blessing.

Consider this verse that just about every Muslim knows:

> *"And remember! your Lord caused to be declared (publicly): 'If ye are grateful, I will add more (favours) unto you...'"*
>
> (Qur'an 14:7)

---

**ISLAMIC VS. SECULAR MANIFESTATION**

Secular Manifestation:
- "I create my reality"
- Trust the universe
- Focus on personal desires Islamic

Islamic Manifestation:
- "Allah creates all reality"
- Trust Allah alone
- Align desires with divine will
- Combine effort with surrender
- Use blessings to serve others

---

This isn't positive thinking—it's divine promise. When we practice *shukr* (gratitude), we're not attracting abundance through cosmic magnetism; we're opening our hearts to receive from *Al-Wahhab* (The Bestower) who owns all treasures.

The Islamic framework for achieving our heart's desires has always existed, woven through practices you already know:

- *Du'a (supplication)*—direct conversation with Allah, not wishful thinking sent into a void
- *Tawakkul* (Trust and reliance on Allah)—taking action while surrendering outcomes to divine wisdom
- *Niyyah (intention)*—purifying our motivations to seek Allah's pleasure first
- *Sabr (patience)*—trusting Allah's timing over our own urgency
- *Shukr (gratitude)*—the spiritual key that multiplies blessings

What we're doing in this book is reclaiming these sacred practices from the shadow of secular self-help. We're returning to the source.

Where others say, "Ask the universe," we turn to Allah in prayer. Where they preach the "law of attraction," we practice the law of divine alignment. Where they promise personal power, we offer something far greater: partnership with the One who controls all power.

> *"And whoever is mindful of Allah, He will make a way out for them, and provide for them from sources they could never imagine."*
> (Qur'an 65:2–3)

Notice the promise: not just provision, but provision from unimaginable sources. Divine alignment transcends vision boards and affirmations. It's about aligning our deepest desires with Allah's will, then witnessing as He opens doors we didn't even know existed.

This is your inheritance as a Muslim—a complete system for spiritual and worldly success that doesn't require you to compromise your faith or adopt foreign concepts. Everything you need to transform your dreams into du'a, and your du'a into divine response, already exists within your tradition.

The question isn't whether Islamic manifestation works. The question is: Are you ready to practice it with the depth and consistency it deserves?

## RECOGNIZING THE TRUE SOURCE

In contemporary self-help and manifestation circles, you'll often hear the term 'universe' used as a source of provision or a force that responds to your desires. But here's what you need to understand as a Muslim: the universe itself is a creation of Allah, subject to His command and will. It has no independent power to grant or withhold blessings.

When you attribute agency or power to the 'universe,' you're subtly diminishing Allah's role as the sole Creator, Sustainer, and Provider. It can unintentionally lead you toward *shirk* (associating partners with Allah), which is the most grievous sin in Islam.

Think of it this way: Imagine a beautiful garden. While you can appreciate the beauty of the flowers and trees, you recognize that it is the gardener who planted, nurtured, and sustains the garden. Similarly, while you can appreciate the wonders of the universe, you must remember that it is Allah who created and sustains it.

This understanding isn't theoretical for me—it's deeply personal. Life has tested me. I've faced trials and tribulations that shook me, yet also shaped me. Some of the most challenging moments became defining moments—turning points that brought me closer to Allah and helped me realign with my purpose.

Over the past few decades, I've developed a practice of starting nearly every morning with meditation and reflection. Before I engage with the outside world, I center myself through stillness. In recent years, I have incorporated *dhikr* (remembrance of Allah) and gratitude into my morning routine.

My du'a always begins the same way: by thanking Allah for the blessings I already have. I am not wealthy in the material sense, but I am living the life I once only envisioned. I reside in the home I prayed for, drive the car I hoped for, travel to places I dreamed about, and, most importantly, have control over my time. I have time to invest in the relationships and community that is important to me. I'm not chasing abundance—I'm living in it because I aligned my heart with the One who provides.

## ALLAH AS AR-RAZZAQ: THE ULTIMATE REALITY

*Ar-Razzaq* is one of Allah's beautiful names, meaning The Provider, The Sustainer. It signifies that Allah is the source of all provision, both material and spiritual. He provides for every creature, from the smallest insect to the largest whale, and He does so with infinite wisdom and mercy.

Your *rizq* (provision bestowed by Allah) isn't limited to money or material possessions. It encompasses everything you need to thrive: health, knowledge, family, peace of mind, opportunities, and guidance. Allah provides rizq in ways you can see and in ways that He hides. He is the Sustainer of all creation. He has already accounted for every living being in His divine record:

> *"There is no moving creature on earth but its sustenance*
> *dependeth on Allah: He knoweth the time and place of its*
> *definitive abode*
> *and its temporary deposit: All is in a clear Record."*
> (Qur'an 11:6)

This provision isn't random—He has measured it with perfect wisdom. Sometimes it's expanded. Sometimes, He withholds it as a mercy or a test.

> *"Say: 'Verily my Lord enlarges and restricts the Sustenance*
> *to such*
> *of his servants as He pleases: and nothing do ye spend in the*
> *least*

*(in His cause) but He replaces it: for He is the Best of those who grant Sustenance.'"*
(Qur'an 34:39)

When you truly believe that Allah is Ar-Razzaq, it transforms how you approach your life. You turn to Him in times of need, seek His guidance in your endeavors, and express gratitude for His blessings. You recognize that your efforts are only a means, and the outcome is in His hands.

Living this reality requires more than internal conviction—it demands that we align our language with our religion. The words we use to describe our goals, dreams, and spiritual practices either reinforce our dependence on Allah or subtly erode it.

## THE LANGUAGE WE USE MATTERS

You need to be careful with language that implies ultimate power or control rests with you rather than with Allah, the Creator and Sustainer of all things.

In this book, when we speak of manifesting, we do not mean that:

- You "create" your reality independently
- The universe "gives" you what you want
- Your thoughts *alone* bring things into being

Instead, we're talking about something far more moving and more sacred: Turning your dreams into du'as, taking action with integrity, and trusting that Allah responds in the best way at the best time.

To reflect this, you'll see the following phrases used throughout this book in place of common manifestation terminology:

| Popular Manifestation Language | Islamic Paradigm |
|---|---|
| Ask the universe | Call upon Allah |
| Attract abundance | Seek rizq from Ar-Razzaq |
| Energy alignment | Align with Allah's will through obedience and intention |

| Create your reality | Surrender your goals to Allah and walk in trust |
| :---: | :---: |
| Raise your vibration | Increase your *taqwa* (God-consciousness) and gratitude |
| The universe provides | Allah is the Only Provider (Ar-Razzaq) |

As a believer, Allah calls you to dream, to strive, to hope—but always with the deep humility that everything you have comes from Allah, not from your own hands alone.

This principle isn't meant to be a once-learned concept but a lived reality, woven into the fabric of daily worship. Consider that in every *rak'ah* (unit of prayer consisting of standing, bowing, and prostrating) of every prayer, you declare:

> *"Thee do we worship, and Thine aid we seek."*
> (Qur'an 1:5)

A Muslim observing the five daily prayers repeats this fundamental truth 17 times each day. Through this constant repetition, our understanding of Allah as the sole source of aid and provision becomes deeply embedded in our consciousness, shaping how we approach every goal and aspiration.

## LIVING THIS REALITY

Relying on Allah for provision isn't passive—it's a state of trust supported by effort and grounded in tawakkul. When you show up with sincerity and trust, Allah provides—often in ways you never imagined. The Prophet (PBUH) said:

> *"If you were to rely upon Allah with the reliance He is due, you would be given provision like the birds: They go out empty stomachs in the morning and return full at dusk."*
> (*Jami' at-Tirmidhi*, Book of Zuhd, Hadith 2344)

This hadith emphasizes the importance of tawakkul—trusting in Allah while still making an effort. Let your daily actions be grounded in that sacred trust. Like the birds, take flight each morning—do your part—knowing that what Allah has written for you will surely return to you.

Sometimes, Allah provides for you in ways that are so unexpected and perfectly timed that they leave no room for doubt. These moments are a compelling reminder that He is always near, always watching over you, and always ready to answer your needs. I experienced this firsthand when my car brokedown.

## REAL STORY OF ALLAH'S UNEXPECTED PROVISIONS

I had just moved to a new, fairly rural city and didn't know anyone. To get to my townhouse, you had to drive past seemingly endless cornfields before entering the new development. It was *Ramadan* (month of fasting), and I was feeling particularly alone in this new place.

One evening, I was running a quick errand before it was time to break my fast. I made the mistake of not bringing water with me. As fate would have it, my car broke down on a rural road. I was feeling a surge of panic when a kind man in a truck stopped and helped me push my car out of the middle of the road.

I called for roadside assistance, but as I waited, the sun began to set. The feeling of isolation was intense. Then Sam (whom I didn't know at the time) rolled down his window and asked if I needed help. Reluctant to accept help from a stranger, I said no. Then my neighbor Eddie rode by, stopped, and waited with me to make sure I was safe. Shortly after, Sam circled back and asked, 'You sure you don't need any help?' I laughed and said, 'Well, not unless you're a mechanic!' To my surprise, he said, 'As a matter of fact, I am.' It turned out that he worked for the dealership of the same make as my car.

Just as it was time to break my fast, the first man who had helped me push the car reappeared. He rolled down his window and handed me a bottle of water.

The story doesn't end there. The next morning, I was scheduled to travel to the airport, which was 90 minutes away. I was worried about how I would get there. My neighbor was also traveling in that direction and offered me a ride to the airport! When I returned, Sam fixed my car. He maintained my vehicle the entire time I lived there.

Looking back, it's clear to me that Allah orchestrated every detail of that experience. When you feel most alone and helpless, Allah is often preparing to send you help from sources you never imagined. It reinforced my belief that He is truly Ar-Razzaq, the Provider, and that He answers your needs in ways that are both timely and perfectly suited to your circumstances.

Experiences like these increase my *iman* (faith). I imagine the questions that I might be asked in the next world, if I were ever to show signs of disbelief in this life:

- Why did you doubt that your Lord was with you?
- Did He not send you water to break your fast?
- A mechanic when you were stranded?
- A ride when you needed one?

Allah sends us signs—not just to test us, but to reaffirm His presence, His nearness, and His mercy.

## THE UNDERSTANDING THAT ALLAH IS THE PROVIDER BRINGS

Understanding Allah as Ar-Razzaq intellectually is one thing. Living this reality in your daily spiritual practice is another. When you genuinely believe Allah is your only source, it transforms:

- How you make du'a (with confidence and trust)
- How you approach your goals (with effort balanced by surrender)

- How you handle delays or obstacles (with patience and faith)
- How you receive blessings (with gratitude and responsibility)

However, believing this truth requires more than intellectual understanding—it necessitates developing spiritual practices that reinforce this reality every day.

Everything you seek—peace, purpose, provision—already belongs to Allah. Ask from the Source, not the creation. When you recognize Allah as Ar-Razzaq, the Provider of all things, you free yourself from the anxiety of depending on limited sources and instead rely on the One whose mercy and provision are infinite.

## SPIRITUAL TAKEAWAY

Understanding Allah as Ar-Razzaq intellectually is one thing. Living this reality in your daily spiritual practice is another. When you genuinely believe Allah is your only source, it transforms, how you speak, make du'a, approach your goals, handle delays, and receive blessings. Everything you seek—peace, purpose, provision—already belongs to Allah. Ask from the Source, not the creation.

## JOURNEY PROMPTS

1. Where in your life have you been attributing power to created things rather than the Creator? How might this be affecting your spiritual practice?
2. Reflect on a time when you achieved something through your own effort. How did you acknowledge Allah's role in that success? How might you approach similar goals differently now with this understanding of Allah as Ar-Razzaq?
3. Write about a time when Allah unexpectedly provided for you. How did this experience deepen your understanding of His names Ar-Razzaq and *Al-Karim* (The Most Generous)?

## As We Continue the Journey

As a Muslim, you already intellectually know that you won't find what you seek in the universe—you find it in the One who created it. But this understanding raises an important question: Since Allah is truly the source of all provision, why do so many people seem to find success through secular methods?

The answer lies in Allah's wisdom, which we cannot fully comprehend. Allah provides through all means according to His divine plan. Sometimes He allows people to gain in this world through various methods, but true success encompasses both *dunya* (this life) and *akhirah* (the next life). When you acknowledge Allah as the Source, your achievements become sustainable, meaningful, and spiritually enriching—benefiting you in both worlds rather than just providing temporary material satisfaction.

In the next chapter, we'll explore how to build the spiritual foundation that ensures your manifestation practice remains authentically Islamic, drawing you closer to Allah rather than away from Him.

## Du'a

*"Ya Allah, guide me to understand the true nature of manifestation through Your divine wisdom. Help me distinguish between what draws me closer to You and what takes me away. Let my dreams and aspirations always be rooted in seeking Your pleasure and aligned with Your will. You are Ar-Razzaq, and I seek only from You."*

"And they have been commanded
no more than this: To worship
Allah, offering Him sincere
devotion, being true (in faith); to
establish regular prayer; and to
practice regular charity; and that is
the Religion Right
and Straight."
(Qur'an 98:5)

# CHAPTER TWO
## BUILDING YOUR ISLAMIC FOUNDATION

Before diving into the manifestation framework, we will establish the spiritual foundation that will keep your practice authentically Islamic. Think of this as preparing good soil before planting seeds. Without the proper foundation, even the best intentions can lead you astray.

## THE CORNERSTONE: TAWHEED (ONENESS OF ALLAH)

Everything in Islamic manifestation begins and ends with the fundamental truth we hold as Muslims: Allah alone has power, Allah alone provides, and Allah alone deserves our worship.

This fundamental truth isn't just theology—it's the practical foundation for how you approach your goals:

- When you want something, you ask Allah, not "the universe"
- When you're grateful, you thank Allah, not cosmic forces
- When you trust the process, you trust Allah's wisdom, not abstract energy

Keeping *Tawheed* (Oneness of Allah) at the center prevents you from accidentally slipping into practices that compromise your faith. Every goal, every method, and every spiritual practice must pass this simple test: Does this center Allah, or does it center something else?

This foundational understanding shapes how you approach every aspect of Islamic manifestation, starting with the most essential practice: du'a.

# DU'A: YOUR DIRECT LINE TO ALLAH

The Prophet (PBUH) said: "Du'a is worship." (*Jami' at-Tirmidhi*, Book of Supplications, Hadith 3372). This statement underscores that your supplications are not mere requests, but a meaningful act of establishing a personal connection with your Creator.

Why *du'a* (supplication) is central to Islamic manifestation:
- It acknowledges Allah as the source of all provision
- It expresses your dependence on divine guidance
- It purifies your intentions and desires
- It builds your relationship with Allah through regular conversation

The difference this makes: You're not sending your hopes into the air, unsure of who's listening. You're having a direct, personal conversation with the One who sees, hears, and responds. This isn't wishful thinking—it's worship.

# PRAYER: YOUR FIVE DAILY RESET POINTS

While du'a can be made at any time and doesn't require formal prayer to be spiritually powerful, your five daily prayers offer natural rhythms for realigning your intentions and maintaining perspective on your goals.

Using *salah* (prayer) to Ground and Guide Your Manifestation Practice
- Before prayer: Reflect on the goals and dreams you want to bring before Allah in du'a
- During prayer: Include brief, specific supplications about your aspirations while in *sujud* (prostration), when you're closest to Allah
- After prayer: Take a moment to consider how your plans align with what pleases Allah and seek His guidance for your next steps

The Blessing of Bringing Salah Into Your Manifestation Journey: Rather than treating manifestation as separate from your spiritual life, this approach weaves your goals and dreams into the worship rhythm you already maintain. Your du'a practice becomes naturally embedded in your daily connection with Allah, strengthening both your spiritual discipline and your clarity about what you're seeking.

## STAYING WITHIN ISLAMIC BOUNDARIES

As you work toward your goals, certain principles will keep you on the straight path:

- Halal means and halal ends: Both what you want and how you pursue it must be permissible in Islam. The success achieved through compromising Islamic values isn't real success—it may bring temporary worldly gain but result in spiritual loss. As the Qur'an reminds us:

> *"What is the life of this world but amusement and play? but verily the Home in the Hereafter,- that is life indeed, if they but knew."*
> (Qur'an 29:64)

- Ethical conduct: Your character during the journey matters as much as reaching your destination. How you treat others while pursuing your goals reflects your Islamic values.
- Balance of *dunya* (this world) and *akhirah* (the next life): Worldly goals are permissible when they don't distract you from spiritual obligations. Your success should draw you closer to Allah, not further away.
- Community responsibility: Your achievements should benefit others and strengthen the *ummah* (Muslim community), not just serve your desires.

As you strive to stay within Islamic boundaries, it's equally important to be aware of what to avoid. Many popular manifestation practices may seem harmless but can quietly steer you off the straight path. Let's look at some of the most common pitfalls—and how to recognize them.

## How To Avoid Common Pitfalls

Certain practices popular in manifestation culture conflict with Islamic principles:

- Seeking guidance from created things: Astrology, tarot, crystal healing, or other divination practices, claim knowledge of the unseen. However, this knowledge is exclusive to Allah.
- Attributing power to yourself: Beliefs like "I create my own reality" or "I am the universe" border on shirk by giving yourself divine attributes.
- Ritualistic practices without Islamic basis: Ceremonies, energy work, or spiritual practices borrowed from other religions may seem harmless but can gradually pull you away from pure Islamic practice.
- Trust in anything other than Allah: Whether it's "universal energy," "higher self," or cosmic forces, Islamic manifestation centers trust exclusively on Allah.

Avoiding what is harmful is part of the path—but so is building habits that bring you closer to Allah. To help you stay spiritually grounded, here's a simple daily rhythm you can begin practicing right away.

## A Simple Foundation Practice

To ground yourself in authentic Islamic manifestation:

- Morning: Begin with "*Bismillah*" (In the name of Allah) and set your intention to seek Allah's pleasure in all your endeavors today.
- Throughout the day: Make brief du'a when you think of your goals: "Ya Allah, if this is good for me, make it easy. If it's not, redirect me to what's better."
- Evening: Thank Allah for the day's blessings and ask forgiveness for any moments when you forgot to center Him in your pursuits.

This simple rhythm keeps Allah at the center of your manifestation practice while building the spiritual habits that will support your journey.

## SPIRITUAL TAKEAWAY

Authentic Islamic manifestation isn't about adding Islamic language to secular practices. It's about approaching your goals through the spiritual framework that Allah has already provided for you. When your foundation is solid, built on Tawheed, du'a, and Islamic boundaries, the manifestation principles in this book become natural expressions of your faith rather than foreign concepts you're trying to make Islamic.

## JOURNEY PROMPTS

1. What aspects of popular spirituality have you been drawn to that might need to be filtered through Islamic principles?
2. Write a personal mission statement that reflects your Islamic values and worldly goals. How can they work together rather than compete?
3. This week, add one specific du'a about your goals after each salah. Keep it consistent and heartfelt.

## AS WE CONTINUE THE JOURNEY

Now that we've established the spiritual foundation that keeps your practice authentically Islamic, it's important to strengthen your spiritual discernment. While many goal-setting principles are universal, the spiritual framework behind them matters deeply. In the next chapter, we'll examine how popular manifestation culture can subtly conflict with Islamic principles, helping you develop the discernment to embrace what serves your faith while avoiding what compromises it.

# DU'A

*"Ya Allah, strengthen my foundation in Tawheed. Help me center You in every aspect of my manifestation journey. Guide me to practices that draw me closer to You and protect me from anything that compromises my faith. Make my spiritual foundation unshakeable."*

"They plot and plan,
and Allah too plans;
but the best of planners
is Allah."
(Qur'an 8:30)

# CHAPTER THREE

As a Muslim developing spiritual discernment, you'll inevitably encounter manifestation culture and New Age spirituality that, while addressing real human needs—purpose, healing, connection—can also blur the crucial line between belief in the Divine and belief in yourself as a divine force.

Developing spiritual discernment isn't just important—it's essential for maintaining the purity of your faith while navigating a culture saturated with spiritual concepts that may conflict with Islamic principles.

## THE FUNDAMENTAL PROBLEM: MISPLACED POWER

The core issue with New Age spirituality isn't the desire for growth or positive change—it's where ultimate power and agency are placed. Consider these common beliefs and their Islamic alternatives:

### 1. "TRUST THE UNIVERSE" VS. TRUSTING ALLAH

New Age Approach: The universe responds to your energy and intentions.

Islamic Approach: Allah created and controls the universe; He alone responds to du'a.

> *"Verily your Lord is Allah, who created the heavens and the earth in six days, and is firmly established on the throne (of authority), regulating and governing all things."*
> (Qur'an 10:3)

## 2. "I CREATE MY REALITY" VS. SURRENDERING TO DIVINE WILL

**New Age Approach:** Your thoughts and mental power manifest your desires.

**Islamic Approach:** You are Allah's servant (abd), not master of creation; your efforts are means, but outcomes belong to Allah.

> *"But they plan, and Allah plans.*
> *And Allah is the best of planners."*
> (Qur'an 8:30)

This misplaced power manifests in several dangerous ways, but perhaps the most subtle and spiritually destructive is the elevation of the self to divine status.

## THE DANGER OF SELF-DEIFICATION

Perhaps the most dangerous pitfall in New Age thought is the subtle deification of the self—believing that you are a god-like being with unlimited potential to create your reality. This directly contradicts the Islamic concept of *ubudiyyah* (servitude to Allah).

Here's the difference in mindset:

- **Ego-based manifestation says:** "I deserve this because I want it."
- **Faith-based manifestation says:** "I ask this of Allah, if it is good for me."

The former centers yourself; the latter surrenders to Divine wisdom.

While you should absolutely strive to develop your potential and use your talents for good, this must always be done with humility and gratitude to Allah. Recognize that all your abilities and blessings come from Him, and you should use them in ways that please Him—not to elevate yourself to His level.

## The Islamic Antidote to Self-Deification

The antidote to self-deification is remembering your true position as Allah's servant (abd). When New Age practices elevate you to creator status—"I manifest my reality," "I am the universe"—Islam grounds you in humility. *Niyyah* (intention) reminds you that even your intentions must be aligned with Allah's pleasure, not your ego's desires. *Du'a* (supplication) keeps you in the posture of asking, not commanding. *Tawakkul* (trust and reliance on Allah) teaches you to trust Allah's plan over your own will. These practices protect you from the spiritual arrogance that comes from believing you have god-like powers to control reality.

Beyond self-deification, New Age spirituality promotes another form of shirk: seeking from created things knowledge that belongs only to Allah.

## Seeking Guidance from Created Things vs. Divine Guidance

New Age Approach: Astrology, tarot, energy readings provide spiritual insight.
Islamic Approach: Only Allah has knowledge of the unseen; seek guidance through Qur'an, Sunnah, and Istikhara.

One of the most seductive aspects of New Age spirituality is the promise of accessing hidden knowledge about your future, purpose, or decisions. Astrology claims the stars determine your personality and fate. Tarot readings suggest cards can reveal what's coming. Psychics offer to connect you with deceased loved ones or predict future events. Crystal ball gazing, numerology, palm reading—all promise to unveil mysteries that feel just beyond your reach.

The appeal is understandable. Life is uncertain, and we desperately want clarity about important decisions: Should I take this job? Will this relationship work? What's my life purpose? When facing crossroads, the human heart craves guidance, and these practices seem to offer immediate answers.

But here's the fundamental problem: these practices attribute knowledge of the unseen (al-ghaib) to created things—stars, cards, crystals, or human intuition. In Islam, knowledge of the unseen belongs exclusively to Allah.

> *"Say: None in the heavens or on earth,*
> *except Allah, knows what is hidden."*
> (Qur'an 27:65)

When you seek guidance from astrology or tarot, you're essentially asking created things to tell you what only the Creator knows. This isn't just spiritually risky—it can become a form of shirk, attributing divine knowledge to something other than Allah.

## THE ISLAMIC ALTERNATIVE

Allah hasn't left you without guidance. He's provided multiple means for seeking direction:

- The Qur'an offers timeless wisdom for life's challenges
- The Sunnah provides prophetic example for decision-making
- Istikhara is a specific prayer for seeking Allah's guidance when facing choices
- Consultation with righteous people who can offer Islamically-grounded advice
- Following Islamic principles that provide clear moral direction

Instead of asking the stars about your future, ask the One who created them. Instead of seeking predictions from cards, seek guidance from the One who controls all outcomes.

These philosophical problems translate into specific practices that Muslims should approach with caution. Let's examine some of the most common ones and their Islamic alternatives.

# SPECIFIC PRACTICES TO APPROACH WITH CAUTION

## ENERGY WORK AND AURA PRACTICES

Energy work includes practices like Reiki (channeling "universal energy" for healing), chakra balancing (working with supposed energy centers), and crystal healing. Aura practices involve reading, cleansing, or protecting the "energy field" that practitioners claim surrounds each person.

From an Islamic perspective, the unseen world contains beings of light (angels) and smokeless fire (jinn). While energy work might seem harmless and may even offer some perceived benefits, some scholars suggest careful discernment, as these practices could potentially open doors to influences that may not align with your spiritual wellbeing. Like alcohol and gambling, which the Qur'an acknowledges contain "some profit, for men; but the sin is greater than the profit" (Qur'an 2:219), the spiritual risks of energy work and aura practices may outweigh any advantages.

Islamic alternatives: Instead of energy work, seek spiritual healing through Qur'anic recitation (ruqyah), *dhikr* (remembrance of Allah) for spiritual purification, and protective du'as—practices that invite Allah's healing and protection while keeping you safe from harmful spiritual influences. For physical ailments, Islam encourages seeking medical treatment, acupuncture, reflexology, and other physical therapies, as Allah has placed healing in these means, while also making du'a for *shifa* (healing) and using prophetic remedies like honey and black seed.

## MIND-OVER-MATTER MANIFESTATION

While positive thinking and clear intentions are valuable, the New Age belief that you can manifest anything solely through mental power crosses into dangerous territory. This includes practices like treating vision boards as magical tools that automatically attract desires, believing that thoughts alone create reality, or using affirmations that center the self rather than Allah.

Popular manifestation culture teaches that if you just think positively enough, visualize clearly enough, or believe strongly enough, you can bend reality to your will. This mind-over-matter approach puts human consciousness in the driver's seat of creation, essentially making you a co-creator with—or replacement for—the Divine.

From an Islamic perspective, this can lead to *ujub* (self-conceit) and spiritual arrogance that displeases Allah. It encourages the belief that your mental power, rather than Allah's will, determines outcomes. When these techniques "work," people credit their own mental abilities. When they don't work, they blame themselves for not believing hard enough, creating a cycle of spiritual pride or self-condemnation.

Islamic Approach: Cultivate positive thoughts and intentions while recognizing Allah as the ultimate source of all power and outcomes. Use visualization to clarify your du'a, not to command the universe. Practice gratitude and optimism as forms of worship, knowing that Allah loves a hopeful, trusting heart while maintaining complete dependence on His will for all results.

Rather than completely avoiding beneficial concepts like goal-setting and self-improvement, the key is reframing them within authentic Islamic principles.

## PRACTICAL REFRAMING

Instead of abandoning the beneficial aspects of goal-setting and visualization, reframe them within Islamic principles:

| New Age Practice | Islamic Alternative |
| --- | --- |
| Visualization to "manifest" | Visualization to enhance and clarify your du'a |
| Self-empowerment affirmations | Qur'anic verses and dhikr that remind you of Allah's attributes |
| "Energy cleansing" rituals | Istighfar (seeking forgiveness) and purifying your niyyah |

| "Raising your vibration" | Increasing your taqwa (God-consciousness) and gratitude |
|---|---|

Understanding why these ideas appeal to people—including Muslims—helps us respond with compassion rather than judgment when we encounter them in our communities.

## WHY THESE IDEAS APPEAL AND THE ISLAMIC RESPONSE

New Age spirituality addresses genuine human needs that every person experiences, regardless of their faith background. Understanding these needs helps us respond with wisdom rather than dismissal.

The Universal Human Needs:

- Feeling empowered in your own life - We all want to believe our choices matter and that we can influence our circumstances
- Practical tools for managing anxiety - In an uncertain world, people seek methods to find peace and control their worries
- Deeper spiritual connection - The human soul naturally craves relationship with the Divine and meaning beyond material existence
- Hope for positive transformation - Everyone desires the possibility of growth, change, and better circumstances

These are not selfish or shallow desires—they reflect the *fitrah* (natural disposition) that Allah placed within every human being. The problem isn't the longing itself, but where people turn to fulfill it.

The Islamic Response:

As Muslims, we can address all these needs through our rich spiritual tradition without compromising our core beliefs. The Qur'an and Sunnah provide comprehensive guidance that surpasses anything New Age spirituality offers:

- For Empowerment: Islam teaches that your choices do matter, but within Allah's sovereignty. You have free will and responsibility (making you genuinely empowered) while maintaining humility before the Ultimate Authority.

- For Anxiety Management: Islamic practices like *dhikr* (remembrance of Allah), *salah* (prayer), *du'a* (supplication), and trust in Allah's plan provide proven methods for finding peace. The five daily prayers alone offer built-in anxiety relief throughout the day.

- For Spiritual Connection: Direct relationship with Allah through prayer, Qur'an reading, and remembrance offers the deepest possible spiritual connection—one that doesn't require intermediaries, crystals, or special abilities.

- For Transformation: Islam's emphasis on personal growth (tazkiyah), seeking forgiveness, and striving for excellence (ihsan) provides a complete framework for positive change grounded in divine guidance rather than self-will.

The beauty of the Islamic response is that it fulfills these needs more completely than New Age alternatives while drawing you closer to truth rather than away from it.

This understanding becomes especially important when dealing with friends and family members who may be drawn to these practices.

## ENGAGING WITH FRIENDS AND FAMILY INVOLVED IN NEW AGE PRACTICES

If you have friends or family members involved in New Age spirituality, approach the topic with compassion and wisdom:

1. Listen and understand: Try to understand what drew them to these practices.

2. Share your perspective: Explain your concerns gently, focusing on the Islamic concept of Tawheed.

3. Offer alternatives: Introduce them to Islamic practices that address their needs, such as dhikr for anxiety or du'a for personal empowerment.

4. Lead by example: Demonstrate how Islamic spirituality enriches your life.
5. Be patient: Remember that guidance comes from Allah. Your role is to convey the message with kindness.

Ultimately, the goal isn't to criticize others but to recognize the complete spiritual system we already possess.

## YOUR SPIRITUAL INHERITANCE

While New Age spirituality may offer appealing concepts and practices, as a Muslim, you have a comprehensive spiritual system that provides more profound, more meaningful ways to connect with the Divine and improve your life. By grounding yourself in Islamic teachings and practices, you can achieve true spiritual growth and manifestation in a manner that aligns with your faith and deepens your relationship with Allah.

You don't need to look outside Islam for spiritual empowerment. Everything you need for growth, healing, and success is already within your faith tradition. The key is to deepen your understanding and practice of authentic Islamic spirituality while remaining discerning about external influences that may divert you from the straight path.

## SPIRITUAL TAKEAWAY

Not everything that sounds spiritual is rooted in truth. Be vigilant about the source of your practices—let your compass be Qur'an and Sunnah. True spiritual empowerment comes from submission to Allah, not from believing you have independent power to control your reality.

## JOURNEY PROMPTS

1. What spiritual practices, beliefs, or energy healing practices outside of Islam have you been drawn to, and how do they align or conflict with Tawheed?

2. Do you catch yourself saying "the universe will provide" instead of "Allah will provide," or using phrases like "it's karma"? What other phrases might you need to reframe?
3. Which of your personal development sources center Allah versus promoting self-empowerment without divine acknowledgment?
4. Are there any spiritual practices that might conflict with pure Islamic monotheism that you find difficult to release, and why? How can you bring these concerns to Allah in du'a?

## AS WE CONTINUE THE JOURNEY

Now that you understand the importance of keeping your manifestation practice rooted in authentic Islamic spirituality, you're ready to explore the practical framework that will guide your journey. You've established the foundation—Allah as the Only Source. You've learned to recognize and avoid spiritual pitfalls.

In the next chapter, we'll start with the first step that transforms vague hopes into focused spiritual intention: learning to visualize with *taqwa*—God-consciousness—rather than ego, and setting your *niyyah* with the clarity and sincerity that invites divine response.

## DU'A

*"Ya Allah, protect me from all forms of shirk, both obvious and subtle. Grant me the wisdom to recognize practices that compromise Tawheed and the strength to avoid them. Keep my heart pure in its devotion to You alone, and guide me always to what pleases You."*

"Verily, this is My way, leading straight: follow it: follow not (other) paths: they will scatter you about from His (great) path: thus doth He command you. that ye may be righteous."
(Qur'an 6:153)

# INTERLUDE
## FROM FOUNDATION TO FRAMEWORK

You've spent the first part of this journey establishing something crucial: a foundation built on Tawheed, not trends. You've focused on Allah as Ar-Razzaq, the Only Source. You've identified the subtle ways New Age thinking can compromise pure Islamic belief. You've begun to see how gratitude, intention, and divine trust have always existed in our tradition—long before they became buzzwords in manifestation culture.

But perhaps you're feeling a gentle tension building. You understand the concepts. You believe in Allah's infinite mercy and provision. You've even started catching yourself when you slip into "universe" language, returning instead to "Ya Allah."

Yet, knowing and doing are different things. Maybe you're wondering: *How do I actually apply this? Where do I start? What does Islamic manifestation look like in my daily life—not just in theory, but in practice?*

This is precisely where you should be. This questioning isn't doubt—it's readiness.

Part II is where knowledge transforms into practice. In the next six chapters, you'll discover a framework that's both deeply spiritual and refreshingly practical. This framework isn't a rigid formula or a magic recipe. It's a living, breathing approach to aligning your hopes with divine will, rooted in:

1. Prophetic example: How the Prophet (PBUH) himself made du'a, took action, and trusted Allah's plan
2. Spiritual wisdom: Time-tested practices from our tradition that cultivate certainty and surrender

3. Practical application: Clear steps you can implement starting today

You'll learn to:

1. Visualize with taqwa, not ego
2. Ask with the confidence of one speaking directly to the Creator
3. Believe with yaqeen that transforms hope into certainty
4. Act with purpose while maintaining complete trust
5. Trust the process even when you can't see the outcome
6. Surrender your timeline to divine wisdom
7. Receive with the gratitude that invites even more blessings

Each step builds on the last, creating a complete cycle of spiritual alignment. But here's what makes this framework uniquely Islamic: it keeps Allah at the center of every stage. You're not manifesting through your own power—you're aligning with His.

## A NOTE BEFORE WE BEGIN

Some of what you'll learn might feel familiar if you've studied personal development before. That's because truth is truth, regardless of who speaks it. But you'll notice crucial differences in the *why* and *how* behind each practice.

Where others say, "raise your vibration," we increase our *taqwa* (God-consciousness). Where they say "trust the process," we trust Allah's plan. Where they celebrate individual achievement, we recognize that every success is from Allah and for serving His creation.

This framework has likely been lived by Muslims throughout history—from companions who built thriving communities in foreign lands to contemporary Muslims navigating modern challenges while maintaining their faith. You're not learning something new; you're reclaiming something that was always yours.

## YOUR INVITATION

As you enter Part II, bring with you:

1. The Islamic foundation you've established
2. Readiness to apply these principles practically
3. Trust in the seven-step process
4. Commitment to keep Allah at the center

Remember: this framework isn't about perfection. It's about progress. You don't need to master every step before moving to the next. Sometimes, you'll find yourself cycling through multiple steps in a single day. That's the beauty of a living practice—it adapts to where you are while guiding you toward where you're meant to be.

The foundation is set. Your heart is prepared. Now, let's discover how to turn your deepest aspirations into a sacred conversation with the Divine—and watch as that conversation transforms your life.

*Bismillah.* Let's begin

# PART TWO
## THE ISLAMIC FRAMEWORK FOR MANIFESTING

*"And if any one puts his trust in Allah, sufficient is (Allah) for him. For Allah will surely accomplish his purpose: verily, for all things has Allah appointed a due proportion."*
(Qur'an 65:3)

"Our Lord! (they say),
Let not our hearts deviate now
after Thou hast guided us, but grant
us mercy from Thine own
Presence; for Thou art
the Grantor of bounties without
measure.
(Qur'an 3:8)

# CHAPTER FOUR
## STEP 1 - VISUALIZE WITH TAFAKKUR & NIYYAH

You've probably heard about visualization in manifestation circles—the practice of imagining your goals as if they've already happened. But when you approach visualization as a Muslim, it becomes something deeper and more purposeful than just wishful thinking or mental rehearsal.

Visualization, when rooted in *ikhlas* (sincerity) and complete submission to Allah, isn't an attempt to control outcomes or "manifest" desires. It's an essential spiritual exercise in seeking clarity and aligning your heart with what is pleasing to Him. In Islam, this act of *tafakkur* (Contemplation) paired with *niyyah* (intention) helps you direct your focus, soften your heart, and refine your du'a, always recognizing Allah as the source of all blessings.

The Qur'an affirms the spiritual value of intentional reflection:

> *"Behold! in the creation of the heavens and the earth, and the alternation of night and day,- there are indeed Signs for men of understanding,- Men who celebrate the praises of Allah, standing, sitting, and lying down on their sides, and contemplate the (wonders of) creation in the heavens and the earth, (With the thought): 'Our Lord! not for naught Hast Thou created (all) this! Glory to Thee! Give us salvation from the penalty of the Fire.'"*
> (Qur'an 3:190-191)

This verse tells you that intentional reflection and contemplation of Allah's signs are deeply spiritual acts. They serve as gateways to remembrance, increased sincerity, and complete submission to His will.

While the Qur'an doesn't explicitly instruct you to engage in 'visualization' as it's known today, you can draw upon its teachings on intention (niyyah) and reflection (tafakkur) to understand its potential benefits when used correctly. When you visualize what you're asking Allah for, you're clarifying your niyyah, making it more focused and sincere. This aligns with the principle that deeds are judged by intentions.

Moreover, visualization helps you reflect deeply on the blessing you're seeking and foster *rajaa* (hope) and positive expectation of Allah's response, knowing that He is capable of granting all things.

## THE ISLAMIC DIFFERENCE IN VISUALIZATION

In contrast to secular approaches that emphasize "manifesting" by commanding the universe, you understand that Allah is the sole provider. Visualization, in your Islamic context, is a tool to clarify your du'a, allowing you to approach Allah with greater focus and humility.

When you envision a goal—whether it's a peaceful home, a fulfilling career that benefits others, or a meaningful relationship built on Islamic principles—you're not commanding the universe to comply. You are preparing your heart to speak to Allah with clarity, recognizing that He is the One who grants all blessings. Visualization becomes a lens through which you examine your hopes and anchor them in Allah's beautiful attributes.

> *"Call upon Allah while being certain of being answered."*
> (*Jami' at-Tirmidhi*, Book of Supplications, Hadith 3479)

## VISIONING THE LIFE ALLAH WANTS FOR YOU

Islam not only allows you to dream—it invites you to. But dreaming as a believer means doing so with surrender, not control. It means having hopes tied to your purpose, not your ego. Your dreams are more of a spiritual force when they are born from your *fitrah* (natural disposition) and aimed toward Allah's pleasure.

> *"When My servants ask thee concerning Me, I am indeed close*
> *(to them): I listen to the prayer of every suppliant when he calleth on Me: Let them also, with a will, Listen to My call, and believe in Me: That they may walk in the right way."*
> (Qur'an 2:186)

## DREAMING BIG BUT REMAINING ROOTED

There's no shame in dreaming big. Wanting a fulfilling career, a loving marriage, a beautiful home, or a healthy body isn't selfish—when those dreams are rooted in a desire to live a righteous, purposeful life. The Prophet (PBUH) made du'a for everything—big and small. So can you.

Unlike many secular manifestation models that encourage 'obsessing' over a vision, Islam teaches you to hold your vision gently. You ask Allah to bless you with what is good for you, even if it looks different than what you imagined. This gentle approach can bring a sense of reassurance, knowing that your vision is in the hands of a higher power.

### TIE YOUR DREAMS TO YOUR DEEN (RELIGION)— NOT DETACHED FROM IT.

True *du'a* (supplication) begins with belief—and belief is often strengthened when you can see the shape of what you're asking for. Visualization is how you translate the vague into the vivid, empowering you to approach your Lord with focused sincerity while always remembering that His knowledge is superior and that blessings may come in a different form.

## REAL STORY OF ALLAH'S ABUNDANT RESPONSE

Visualization helps you reflect deeply on the blessing you're seeking. This principle became real for me when I dreamed of working remotely from abroad. I used visualization, not as a magic trick, but as a tool to clarify my intention and connect with Allah. Both living abroad and visiting the great mosques of the world were prominent on my vision board. I pictured:

- Living in another country while serving my clients here
- Experiencing different cultures where most people shared my religion
- Having the freedom to travel and explore
- Visiting the great masjids of the world

Allah gave me more than I asked for. I was able to move to Morocco for two years, and what I received exceeded every expectation. I didn't just live there—I was welcomed into a Moroccan family and became part of their extended family. I celebrated holidays with them and share significant family events. I formed deep friendships with others that continue today, and I connected with an Arabic/ Qur'an teacher who remain very special to me.

Most remarkably, I had envisioned visiting great masjids around the world, but Allah placed me in an apartment directly across from one of the most magnificent mosques in the world-Hassan II Mosque in Casablanca, also known as the the Mosque on the Sea. I had only hoped to visit such places, yet here I was waking up each morning to the call to prayer echoing from this architectural marvel with the sound of the ocean as the accompanying music.

What I received exceeded my expectations, but what mattered most was how the process clarified my values and strengthened my trust in Allah's plan. Every visualization became a supplication, every intention a seed of surrender. *Alhamdulillah* (all praise is due to Allah) for blessings that surpassed my imagination.

## GUIDELINES FOR ISLAMIC VISUALIZATION

Islam allows you to dream. It asks you to dream in the light of *Tawheed* (Oneness of Allah), always remembering that He is the ultimate source. Dream with:

- *Ikhlas* (sincerity): Ensuring that your intentions are pure and solely for the sake of Allah, not for ego or worldly gain
- *Halal* (permissible) aims: Ensuring that the goals you visualize are permissible according to Islamic law and beneficial to yourself and others
- Action and effort: Combining visualization with concrete steps toward your goals, knowing that Allah rewards those who strive with sincerity and diligence

When you approach your dreams with these principles, you remain anchored in a fundamental truth:

> *"And ye have no good thing but is from Allah"*
> (Qur'an 16:53)

## THE SACRED PAUSE BEFORE VISUALIZATION

Before you begin your visualization, take a moment to center yourself. In the Islamic tradition, this can be a form of *tafakkur*—contemplation rooted in remembrance of Allah. Start with a simple meditation that prepares your heart for divine connection.

Simple Islamic Meditation Technique:

1. Set a timer for 5-15 minutes (beginners start with 5, experienced practitioners can extend to 10-15 minutes)
2. Find a quiet space and face the *qiblah* if possible
3. Begin with *Bismillah al-Rahman al-Raheem* - "In the name of Allah, the Most Gracious, the Most Merciful"
4. Close your eyes and breathe deeply, allowing your heart to become still

5. Practice gentle *dhikr* (remembrance of Allah) - choose one of these rhythmic remembrances:
   o "*SubhanAllah*" (glory be to Allah) with each inhale, "*Alhamdulillah*" (all praise is due to Allah) with each exhale
   o "*Allah Hu*" (He is Allah) - breathing "Allah" on the inhale and "Hu" on the exhale, affirming His presence and transcendence
6. Let this be a sacred pause, a moment of presence before the imagining begins

Deepening Your Practice:

Heart-centered awareness: Place your hand over your heart and feel its rhythm. Remember that this heartbeat is sustained by Allah's will—each beat a gift from *Al-Hayy* (The Ever-Living).

Breath as remembrance: Let each breath remind you that you are alive by His will. The Arabic word for soul (*ruh*) and spirit (*rih*, meaning wind) share the same root—connecting your breath to the divine spirit within you.

Sacred silence: As you settle into stillness, practice the meditation technique of the early Muslims: silent contemplation of Allah's attributes. Choose one of His beautiful names—perhaps *Ar-Rahman* (The Most Merciful) or *As-Sabur* (The Patient)—and let it fill your awareness.

Meditation, when done with intention and awareness of Allah, can help quiet the noise of the world and tune you into the deeper whispers of your soul. It's not about emptying your mind but rather filling it with clarity, presence, and divine purpose. You are not alone in this space— Allah is nearer to you than your jugular vein. (Qur'an 50:16)

Let your breath remind you that you are alive by His will. Let your silence become a canvas upon which you begin to envision the life that aligns with your du'a, your faith, and your highest self in service to Him.

# GUIDED VISUALIZATION EXERCISE

Take a moment. Close your eyes. Breathe. Imagine your du'a has already been answered.

Step into that vision:

- What are you wearing?
- What does your daily rhythm feel like?
- Who are you serving, and how?

Step into that version of yourself now. Embody it. Let the energy of that answered prayer shape your actions today. Imagine yourself five years from now—consistent in prayer, grounded in gratitude, anchored in intention. You've grown in *iman* (faith), clarity, and compassion.

Now, gently reflect:

- Where am I?
- What is the pace and purpose of my day?
- Who surrounds me, uplifts me, and believes in me?
- How am I giving back to the world?
- In what ways am I serving with love?
- What fills my heart with gratitude?

Most importantly: Does this vision please Allah? Ask yourself, how can I take a step today to bring myself closer to my vision, in a way that is pleasing to Him?

# FROM VISION TO SACRED SUPPLICATION

Now, shape that vision into a sacred supplication. Ask Allah:

*"Ya Allah, place me exactly where You want me. Surround me with people and provision that support the purpose You created me for. Let my joy be a reflection of Your mercy, and let my success draw me nearer to You."*

This is the essence of Islamic visualization—not demanding outcomes from the universe, but clarifying your heart's desires so you can present them to Allah with sincerity and trust in His perfect wisdom.

## SPIRITUAL TAKEAWAY

*Tafakkur* (contemplation) is a form of worship that brings you closer to Allah. When you visualize with sincerity and set your intention with Allah in mind, you're not just dreaming—you're directing your heart toward Him and preparing yourself to receive what He knows is best for you. It is in the quiet moments of meditation and visualization that you silence the whispers of Shaytan and create sacred space to hear Allah's guidance.

## JOURNEY PROMPTS

1. When you imagine your ideal life, what role does your relationship with Allah play in that vision?
2. How can your personal success become a means of serving Allah and benefiting others?
3. Write a detailed visualization of your life 5 years from now, ensuring each element aligns with Islamic values. Include spiritual, family, career, and service goals.
4. You already have started a practice of spending 5-15 minutes each morning meditating. Now, this week, spend 10 minutes each morning visualizing one of your goals while making it a conversation with Allah about why you want it.

## AS WE CONTINUE THE JOURNEY

You've learned to clarify your vision and purify your intention, creating a crystal-clear picture of what your heart truly seeks. This clarity is revolutionary—but it's only the beginning.

Many people stop here, carrying beautiful intentions that never transform into reality. They visualize, they hope, but they never learn the sacred art that bridges the gap between desire and divine response.

We are about to explore, the most life-changing spiritual practice in Islam—one that the Prophet (PBUH) used for everything from the smallest daily needs to the most momentous life decisions. In the next chapter, we'll unlock the power of du'a, not as a desperate last resort, but as the golden thread that weaves through every aspect of authentic Islamic manifestation.

## DU'A

*"Ya Allah, purify my intentions and help me see with the light of sincerity. Align my vision with Your will, and let my dreams serve Your purpose for my life."*

"When My servants ask thee concerning Me, I am indeed close (to them):
I listen to the prayer of every suppliant when he calleth on Me: Let them also, with a will, Listen to My call, and believe in Me: That they may walk in the right way."
(Qur'an 2:186)

# CHAPTER FIVE
## STEP 2: ASK WITH DU'A

You've clarified your vision and purified your intention. Now comes the most beautiful step in your journey—turning that intention into sacred conversation with your Creator. Asking isn't a sign of weakness—it's an act of worship rooted in sincere intention and trust in Allah's wisdom. This chapter explores how du'a strengthens your connection with Allah, clarifies your hopes, and transforms your longing into spiritual purpose.

## THE SOURCE OF ALL PROVISION

In a world filled with messages to "ask the universe," you need to remember that your true source of sustenance and guidance is Allah alone. The stars, the moon, and cosmic energies don't shape your destiny or manifest your dreams. Only Allah, the Creator, has the power to respond and provide.

When you desire—whether for provision, clarity, or guidance—you call upon Allah's attribute of *Ar-Razzaq* (The Provider). When confusion or uncertainty clouds your path, you seek Allah's guidance as *Al-Hadi* (The Guide). When you hope for better outcomes, you invoke His generosity as *Al-Karim* (The Generous) and His responsiveness as *Al-Mujib* (The One Who Responds).

> **THE 99 BEAUTIFUL NAMES OF ALLAH**
>
> Islam teaches that Allah has 99 beautiful names (Asma ul-Husna) that describe His perfect attributes. When making du'a, Muslims often call upon Allah using these names:
>
> - Ar-Rahman (The Most Merciful)
> - Ar-Razzaq (The Provider)
> - Al-Hakeem (The All-Wise)
> - Al-Ghafoor (The Oft-Forgiving)
>
> Knowing these names deepens your connection with Allah and makes your du'a more meaningful.
>
> You'll find the complete list of the 99 names of Allah and their meaning in the appendix.

These aren't vague energies; they are the beautiful attributes of Allah. Calling upon these qualities during du'a establishes a direct connection to the One who is near, merciful, and capable of fulfilling your needs per His wisdom. As the Prophet (PBUH) said:

*"Du'a is worship."*
(*Jami' at-Tirmidhi,* Book of Supplications, Hadith 3372)

## DU'A IS WORSHIP, NOT WISHFUL THINKING

When you raise your hands in du'a, you're not merely hoping that something might hear you. You're speaking directly to the Creator—The One who fashioned you, knows your needs, and has promised to respond. Du'a is an act of worship, a heartfelt conversation with Allah rooted in humility and trust.

However, intention and clarity are essential. Without intention and clarity your du'as risk becoming vague or insincere. To truly benefit from this divine dialogue, approach it with purpose and mindfulness.

## A DIVINE INVITATION TO ASK

You are here for a reason. Deep within you is a longing—perhaps for peace, clarity, purpose, or ease. That longing isn't random. It's often a divine nudge, a sign that Allah is inviting you to draw closer to Him through your du'a, your seeking, and your trust.

*"Call on Me; I will answer your (Prayer)..."*
(Qur'an 40:60)

## YOUR DREAMS ARE NOT TOO BIG FOR ALLAH

Sometimes you may limit what you ask for. You shrink your du'a. You fear asking for too much because you feel unworthy, you've internalized scarcity, or someone once told you your dreams were unrealistic.

But Allah is not limited, and He doesn't ask you to limit yourself. The Qur'an repeatedly reminds you that the earth is spacious, and His provision is abundant. Your *rizq* isn't dependent on market trends, job offers, or who you know. His *rahmah* (mercy) isn't rationed. When you call upon Him, you're not adding to His burden—you're returning to the Source.

Ask. Ask big. Ask sincerely, not arrogantly, but faithfully. There's no shortage in the kingdom of Allah. Your dreams, your du'as, your longings—when aligned with good intentions—aren't a burden to Him. They're a sign of your connection to Him.

> *"...but my mercy extendeth to all things"*
> (Qur'an 7:156)

## THE MOST GENEROUS RESPONDS

Allah's giving is generous, intentional, and limitless. You can be wealthy in *iman* (faith), gratitude, and impact. Even when seeking worldly provision, what matters most is that your du'a is sincere and your reliance is rooted in *tawakkul* (trust and reliance on Allah).

> *"Verily thy Lord doth provide sustenance in abundance for whom He pleaseth, and He provideth in a just measure. For He doth know and regard all His servants."*
> (Qur'an 17:30)

True provision isn't always material. It includes peace, clarity, and contentment—the kind that no possession can buy.

> *"Wealth is not in having many possessions. Rather, true wealth is contentment of the soul."*
> (*Sahih al-Bukhari*, Book of Manners, Hadith 644, Also recorded in *Sahih Muslim*, Hadith 1051)

And when you turn to Him sincerely, Allah responds not with reluctance, but with mercy and generosity.

> *"Your Lord is munificent and generous and is ashamed to turn away empty the hands of His servant when he raises them to Him."*
> (*Sunan Abi Dawud* 1488, Book 8, Hadith 73)

Trusting in Allah's plan doesn't mean you stop trying. It means you know that your provision will reach you, even from unexpected paths—because He promised it would.

> *"And for those who fear Allah, He (ever) prepares a way out, And He provides for him from (sources) he never could imagine."*
> (Qur'an 65:2-3)

And above all, never fear missing what Allah has set aside for you and Allah is generous.

> *"No soul will die until it has received all its provision..."*
> (*Sunan Ibn Majah*, Book of Zuhd, Hadith 2144)

> *"Call upon Allah while being certain of being answered."*
> (*Jami' at-Tirmidhi*, Book of Supplications, Hadith 3479)

## ASK WITH INTENTION AND CLARITY

These hadith remind you that Allah has already written your provision and eagerly responds to sincere prayer. Other hadith speak to Allah's generosity, encouraging you to approach Him with both trust and specificity. Instead of vague requests—like "Give me more money"—it's more meaningful to ask with clarity and conviction. For example, define what success, peace, or provision means to you.

You're not overwhelming Allah; you're demonstrating your trust in His omniscience by fully investing your heart in your request. Clear, sincere du'a honors His role as the All-Knowing and allows Him to respond in a way that is best for your spiritual growth and worldly needs.

Before you ask, ask yourself why.

- Not: "*I want a house.*"
- Instead: "*Ya Allah, grant me a home filled with peace, where I can worship You with ease, host in Your name, and raise a family in faith.*"

Clarity isn't control. *Tawakkul* (trust and reliance on Allah) guides intention.

## PROVISION IS ALREADY WRITTEN

Allah doesn't merely allow you to ask—He encourages it. Allah reminds you that His provision is broad and generous and often comes from where you least expect it. As Muslims we should never be operating from a place of lack or scarcity.

Scarcity is a tool of Shaytan. He whispers fear into your heart—fear of not having enough, fear of being disappointed, fear that you're asking for too much. But Allah promises bounty. He promises forgiveness. He invites you into a reality where trust opens doors that hustle cannot.

> "*The Evil one threatens you with poverty and bids you to conduct unseemly. Allah promiseth you His forgiveness and bounties.*
> *And Allah careth for all and He knoweth all things.*"
> (Qur'an 2:268)

You're not meant to live in fear. Your path is one of tawakkul. When you rely on Allah as you should, you are sustained—not by your striving alone, but by His mercy. The Prophet (PBUH) said:

*"If you were to rely upon Allah with the reliance He is due,
you would be given provision like the birds: they go out
hungry in the morning and return full in the evening."*
(*Jami' at-Tirmidhi*, Book of Zuhd, Hadith 2344)

Abundance isn't just about more—it's about divine multiplication. Your good intentions, your trust, your giving—Allah meets them all with increase, in both seen and unseen ways.

*"And in heaven is your Sustenance,
as (also) that which ye are promised."*
(Qur'an 51:22)

Allah has already written our provision. You don't have to beg the universe or chase every opportunity in desperation. Seek through tawakkul and obedience, and know that what Allah has for you will reach you, even if it's between two mountains. The Prophet (PBUH) said:

*"No soul will die until it has received all its provision.
So fear Allah and be moderate in seeking it."*
(*Sunan Ibn Majah*, Book 37 (Zuhd), Hadith 2144)

## A REAL STORY OF MANIFESTATION

For me the power of du'a isn't just theology—it's lived reality.

A few months ago, I embarked on a journey to find a new home. Little did I know that this experience would become clear evidence of the effectiveness of sincere and specific du'a, coupled with patience, persistence, and effort.

The third house I viewed, with my new realtor, seemed to materialize straight from my vision board—a physical manifestation of the dreams I had carefully curated. It answered all my needs so perfectly that it almost felt too good to be true. My realtor cautioned me about the competitive nature of this property, emphasizing that if I genuinely wanted it, I needed to be aggressive in my approach.

However, several obstacles loomed before me:

- The house was priced higher than my initial budget
- As a self-employed person, I didn't have conventional income documentation

I turned to du'a—specific, heartfelt, and anchored in trust. I was specific in my asks, visualizing not only owning the house but also how I would use it as a blessing, filling it with family and community. Throughout the process, I stayed in constant prayer, seeking Allah's guidance and responding with patience and effort.

It's important to note that while du'a is effective, patience and persistence are crucial. Results may not always be immediate, and maintaining steadfastness in your supplications is essential. Additionally, I understood that prayer alone isn't a plan. While making du'a, I also took concrete steps toward my goal, embodying the principle of *tawakkul*—reliance on Allah while taking action.

I did my part by saving money before I started house shopping. Once I found my dream house, I thought I might fall short of what I needed— and then Allah provided the rest through a last-minute business opportunity that came my way. I diligently stayed on top of closing deadlines and maintained fair dealings with the seller. This combination of sincere du'a and personal effort proved to be a winning formula.

The results were remarkable:

- A smooth closing
- Positive dealings with the realtor and seller
- A home that is quickly becoming a community hub and a family gathering spot

This experience reinforced for me the power of du'a when coupled with sincere intention (*niyyah*), specific asks, trust in Allah's plan, and personal effort. It served as a vivid reminder that when you turn to Allah with clarity and faith, He can make the seemingly impossible become reality.

## GRATITUDE IN ACTION

Later in this book, I discuss gratitude (shukr) in detail as a cornerstone of Islamic manifestation, but I think it's fitting to mention it here in this context of receiving Allah's provision with proper acknowledgment.

My gratitude to Allah wasn't just verbal but also manifested in action. When we closed, the real estate company presented me with a bottle of champagne. I politely declined, saying, "I don't drink." When they suggested I take it home and pop the bottle in the backyard, I firmly stated, "Absolutely not. I will not thank Allah with alcohol."

Instead, I chose to express my gratitude through actions that aligned with my faith and values. I organized a housewarming gathering two months later to welcome family and close friends, making it my first gathering in the new home. Shortly after *Ramadan* (month of fasting), I held the first sisters' gathering, which I branded as "Sisters' Steadfast Saturdays."

I committed to hosting these gatherings monthly despite not knowing many sisters in the area initially. To my pleasant surprise and as a testament to Allah's blessings, nine sisters attended the first gathering, and the number grew to sixteen for the second. Opening my home is how I chose to show my gratitude—by using the blessing Allah had given me to foster community and sisterhood.

This experience taught me that the power of du'a lies not just in the asking but in the sincere intention, the effort you put forth, and how you use the blessings you receive to benefit others and please Allah. It reinforced the importance of coupling your prayers with action, being patient and persistent in your supplications, and expressing your gratitude in ways that honor your faith and benefit your community.

## CHARITY MULTIPLES

The Qur'an and the Prophet (PBUH) remind us that charity multiplies blessings.

> *The parable of those who spend their substance in the way*
> *of Allah is that of a grain of corn: it groweth seven ears, and*
> *each ear Hath a hundred grains. Allah giveth manifold*
> *increase to whom He pleaseth: And Allah careth for all and*
> *He knoweth all things."*
> (Qur'an 2:261)

Abundance, in an Islamic paradigm, isn't simply about increase—it's about *barakah* (blessing) and multiplication. What you give with sincerity and trust is never lost. The Prophet (PBUH) said:

> *"Charity does not decrease wealth."*
> (*Sahih Muslim*, Book 45 (The Book of Virtue,
> Good Manners, and Joining the Ties of Kinship), Hadith
> 2588)

While giving multiplies your blessings, spiritual purification opens the channels to receive them.

## FORGIVENESS UNLOCKS PROVISION

Before asking for more, cleanse your heart's vessel. The Qur'an associates repentance with blessings in both this life and the next.

> *"Saying, 'Ask forgiveness from your Lord; for He is Oft-*
> *Forgiving;*
> *He will send rain to you in abundance; Give you increase*
> *in wealth and sons; and bestow on you gardens*
> *and bestow on you rivers (of flowing water).'"*
> (Qur'an 71:10-12)

Seeking *istighfar* (forgiveness) and making *tawbah* (repentance) purifies your heart and clears spiritual blocks that may be standing in the way of your du'a. Sometimes, forgiveness is the gateway to provision. By turning to Allah sincerely, you reopen the flow of His mercy and blessings in your life.

# THE STORY OF SEEKING FORGIVENESS AND PROVISION

There's a beautiful narration about Abdullah ibn Mas'ud (may Allah be pleased with him) that illustrates the connection between spiritual clarity and provision. A man came to visit him after having been away for a while. Ibn Mas'ud asked how he was doing, and the man replied that he and his family were well, but financially, he had lost everything.

Ibn Mas'ud lowered his head and remained silent for a long time. Then he raised his head and said, "Bring the Holy Qur'an!" He flipped through it until he came to the verse:

> *"Whoever constantly seeks forgiveness, Allah will create a path*
> *out of every difficulty, remove every worry, and grant them*
> *sustenance from sources they could never imagine."*
> (Qur'an 65:2-3)

Ibn Mas'ud then said to the man, *"I will give you the same advice that Allah gave you. Constantly seek forgiveness from Allah, and improve your relationship with Him!"*

This story reminds you that provision often begins with purifying your relationship with Allah, which includes clarifying your intentions and aligning your heart with His will.

# COME WITH CLEAN HANDS AND A CLEAN HEART

I often reflect on the legal doctrine of "unclean hands" that I learned in my first year of law school—a principle that bars a person from seeking equitable relief if they have acted unjustly or in bad faith. The idea is simple: you cannot ask for justice while acting unjustly yourself. That principle has stayed with me throughout my professional career and personal dealings, and it often comes to mind when I think about du'a— asking Allah for something from the depths of your soul.

When you approach Allah with your requests, how are you showing up? Is your heart sincere? Are your hands ethically clean? Spiritually, the same standard applies: you must come to your Lord with clean hands and a clean heart.

Coming to your Lord clean is one of the wisdom behind *wudu* (ritual ablution), the ritual washing before prayer. You cleanse your outer self—your hands, face, limbs—not just for hygiene but to symbolically and spiritually prepare yourself for divine connection. These are the words of the Prophet:

> *"When a Muslim or a believer washes his face in wudu',*
> *every sin he committed with his eyes is washed away...*
> *when he washes his hands, every sin they handled*
> *is washed away... until he emerges purified from sin."*
> (*Sahih Muslim*, Book of Purification, Hadith 244)

You're taught not even to touch the Qur'an without clean hands. Some people perform wudu before reading the Qur'an. These actions aren't empty rituals—they're signs of reverence that prepare your heart for divine connection. Before you ask Allah for what you need, you purify yourself to the best of your ability—not because you must be perfect, but because you're striving to be sincere.

The state of your heart affects the outcome of your actions:

> *"Truly in the body there is a morsel of flesh which, if it is*
> *sound,*
> *the whole body is sound; and if it is corrupt,*
> *the whole body is corrupt. Truly, it is the heart."*
> (*Sahih al-Bukhari*, Book of Belief, Hadith 52,
> *Sahih Muslim*, Book of Governance, Hadith 1599)

So when you turn to Allah in du'a, you must ask yourself: Am I harboring resentment? Have I wronged others? Am I seeking something righteous, or am I driven by ego or greed? These questions purify your intention and open the way for divine mercy.

The consequences of neglecting this spiritual posture are illustrated in an enlightening hadith. The Prophet (PBUH) tells of a man whose prayers go unanswered despite his apparent desperation:

> *"A man who travels long distances, disheveled and dusty, raises his hands to the sky saying, 'O Lord, O Lord,' while his food is unlawful, his drink is unlawful, his clothing is unlawful, and he is nourished with the unlawful—so how can his supplication be accepted?"*
> (*Sahih al-Bukhari*, Book of Belief, Hadith 52,
> *Sahih Muslim*, Book of Governance, Hadith 1599)

Though this traveler displays all the outward signs of sincere supplication—enduring hardship, calling upon Allah with raised hands—his prayers are blocked by one crucial failing: he sustains himself through unlawful means. The Prophet's rhetorical question drives home the lesson: no amount of apparent devotion can overcome the spiritual barrier created by consuming what is forbidden.

It's not enough to ask. You must ask from a place of ethical alignment and spiritual sincerity. Just as a court of law requires clean hands to make a claim, you approach the Divine court with clean hands and a clean heart, knowing that what you bring in truth, Allah will receive in mercy.

When I say, "Come with clean hands and a clean heart," I'm not saying you must be perfect or free from sin. But the cleaner you come, the more prepared you'll be to receive.

I've walked this path not in perfection, only in pursuit. There were stumbles, wrong turns, and times when it seemed I was off course. *Alhamdulillah* (all praise is due to Allah), I always found my way back, whispering du'a through tears and hope. And somehow, that was enough.

I know my blessings didn't come because I got everything right. I believe they came because I kept showing up—and perhaps because of a deed that I wasn't even aware of, like giving someone ease with a smile.

I kept believing. I kept seeking forgiveness, and Allah kept showing me mercy and responding to my du'as, sometimes giving me what I asked for, sometimes giving me more, and other times denying me what was not best for me. To all I say, "Alhamdulillah".

The lesson from my journey—and what I want you to understand—is that perfection isn't required, but sincerity is everything.

## YOUR SUPERPOWER: SINCERITY

You don't need rituals or charms from other traditions. Your true strength in manifesting is *Ikhlas* (sincerity)—pure sincerity of heart. Even a quiet, heartfelt whisper in the night, if done with pure sincerity, holds more power than grand, performative acts.

## HOW TO ASK ALLAH WITH SINCERITY

Du'a isn't a checklist or routine recitation—it's an intimate conversation with your Creator. The Prophet (PBUH) taught us specific principles that transform ordinary requests into worship. My du'a practice changed completely when I learned these principles.

### 1. Be Clear

Avoid vague statements like, "I want more money." Instead, be specific in your requests to Allah. Specificity refines your intention and reflects trust that Allah hears your every word.

Example: When making du'a for a house, I was specific: a home I could close on with ease, in a Muslim-friendly community, near my preferred masjid, suitable for gatherings, and accessible to the city. I received all of these.

## 2. Be Present

Don't make du'a a checklist. Slow down. Imagine you are in intimate conversation with your Creator—because you are. Let each word carry weight and meaning.

Example: I often made my du'as after salah when I was already in the frame of mind of being present with Allah.

## 3. Be Repetitive

Du'a isn't one-and-done. The Prophet (PBUH) often repeated his supplications. Repetition isn't a sign of doubt; it's devotion. Each repetition can deepen your sincerity and focus.

Example: I made this du'a consistently—after salah, after Jumu'ah, when house-hunting. The repetition kept my heart connected to the request.

# THE SACRED TIMES AND ETIQUETTE OF DU'A

While Allah is always near and ready to listen, certain times and practices can deepen the spiritual power of your supplication. Learning these can transform your du'a practice from routine to sacred encounter.

Etiquette of Du'a

- Begin with praise of Allah and salawat upon the Prophet (PBUH)
- Face the *qiblah*, (direction of prayer) if possible
- Raise your hands in humility
- Ask with sincerity and hope, not entitlement
- End with praise, gratitude, and more salawat

The Most Blessed Times for Du'a

These times aren't just suggestions—they're when the spiritual atmosphere is most receptive

- The last third of the night - when Allah descends to the lowest heaven
- Between the *adhan* (call to prayer) and *iqamah* (call to commence prayer) -moments of anticipation before prayer
- When in *Sujud* (prostration) - the position closest to Allah

- While fasting and at the time of breaking fast - moments of spiritual purification
- On Fridays - especially the last hour before *Maghrib* (sunset prayer)
- On the Day of Arafah - the most sacred day for supplication
- At iftar during Ramadan - when breaking the fast
- During the last 10 nights of Ramadan - especially seeking Laylat al-Qadr
- When it rains - a sign of Allah's mercy descending

The Prophet Muhammad (PBUH) said:

> *"Indeed, your Lord is generous and shy. If His servant raises his hands to Him (in du'a), He becomes shy to return them empty."*
> (*Jami' at-Tirmidhi*, Book of Supplications, Hadith 3556)

Du'a Tip: Create a "Du'a List" for these blessed times. These are moments when the veil between you and Allah feels especially thin.

## WHY CONSISTENCY MATTERS

What's the difference between someone who makes du'a occasionally and someone who maintains daily spiritual dialogue with Allah? Consistency. Regular du'a transforms not just your requests, but your entire relationship with the Divine. The power of du'a lies not just in the asking, but in the strengthening of your relationship with Allah through the process. It's about cultivating a heart that turns to Him in all matters, big and small.

Regular du'a:

- Softens your heart and increases humility
- Builds *yaqeen* (certainty) in Allah's responsiveness
- Develops spiritual discipline and mindfulness

- Creates sacred rhythm in your daily life
- Strengthens your connection to divine guidance

## HOW TO DEEPEN YOUR DU'A PRACTICE

Connecting Your Requests to Allah's Names

When you make du'a, reflect on which of Allah's beautiful names connects with your specific need. For example:

- Ar-Rahman (The Most Merciful) for healing and comfort
- Ar-Razzaq (The Provider) for provision and sustenance
- Al-Hadi (The Guide) for guidance and direction
- As-Sabur (The Patient) when asking for patience
- Al-Fattah (The Opener) for new opportunities

Invoking the names of Allah isn't just a theological idea—it's a spiritual practice with power. Aligning your prayer with His attributes helps focus your heart, deepen your connection, and bring sincerity to your supplication.

Making Du'a for Others

The Prophet (PBUH) said the du'a made for another person in their absence is quickly answered. Include others in your supplications:

- Family and friends
- The Muslim *ummah* (Muslim community)
- Those who are suffering
- Your community and neighbors

## SPIRITUAL TAKEAWAY

Du'a isn't a backup plan—it's your lifeline. When you ask from Allah with presence and humility, you step into a sacred conversation that transforms both your requests and your heart. The power lies not in the words alone but in the sincerity with which you speak them, the trust you place in His response, and the consistency with which you maintain this divine dialogue. Allah loves consistency in small deeds, so let your du'a become a living, breathing rhythm in your relationship with Him.

## JOURNEY PROMPTS

1. What have you been hesitant to ask Allah for, and why? Is it fear, unworthiness, or past disappointment?

2. Which of Allah's 99 names most relates to what you're currently seeking?

3. Write a heartfelt du'a for your biggest dream, being specific about what you want and why. Include how you'll use this blessing to serve Allah.

4. This week, choose one of the blessed times for du'a (last third of the night, between adhan and iqamah, etc.) and make it your consistent practice time.

5. Create a simple daily du'a routine: Choose 1-2 du'as from your personal list to focus on each week, and practice them at the same time each day for consistency.

## AS WE CONTINUE THE JOURNEY

You've discovered the dynamic power of sincere, specific du'a and learned to weave it into the fabric of your daily life. This sacred conversation connects your heart directly to Allah's infinite mercy, creating a living practice that sustains your connection to the Divine.

But establishing a consistent du'a practice is only the foundation. The next crucial element determines whether your supplications become a source of peace or anxiety, confidence or doubt. It's the quality that transforms prayer from hopeful wishing into certain expectation of Allah's response.

Many sincere Muslims make du'a regularly yet still carry uncertainty in their hearts. They ask but wonder if Allah truly hears them. They pray, but doubt whether their requests matter to the Creator of the universe.

This uncertainty creates spiritual restlessness that undermines the very practice meant to bring peace.

The missing element is yaqeen—unshakeable certainty in Allah's attention, care, and response. In our next step, we'll discover how to build the kind of deep, unwavering conviction that transforms hesitant hope into confident trust in Allah's perfect wisdom and timing.

## DU'A

*"Ya Allah, let me never hesitate to turn to You. Open my heart to ask You with clarity, sincerity, and trust. Make my du'a a source of closeness to You and strength for my journey. Help me maintain consistency in my supplications and find peace in Your perfect timing. Let my daily practice of du'a draw me ever closer to You."*

"And if any one puts
his trust in Allah,
sufficient is (Allah) for him. For
Allah will surely accomplish his
purpose:
verily, for all things has Allah
appointed a due proportion."
(Qur'an 65:3)

# CHAPTER SIX
## STEP 3: BELIEVE WITH YAQEEN

You've established a consistent du'a practice. Now comes another crucial elements of your manifestation journey: belief. Not just hoping things might work out but developing *yaqeen* (certainty)—the deep, unshakeable certainty that Allah hears you and will respond in the way that's best for you.

Du'a rooted in yaqeen grows even in unseen soil. When you trust wholeheartedly that Allah hears and responds, your supplications become a reflection of deep reliance, patience, and faith. *Du'a* (supplication) rooted in yaqeen isn't about believing you'll get precisely what you want when you want it—it's about accepting that Allah's response is always perfect, even when you can't see the wisdom yet.

## What Is Yaqeen?

Yaqeen is a deep, unwavering certainty in Allah's plan—even when you can't see the signs. It's the firm belief that the outcome is in Allah's hands and trust that He knows what is best, even if you cannot see the results immediately. Yaqeen means believing, not necessarily in what you see, but in Allah—the All-Knowing and All-Wise.

Think of it this way: Yaqeen means continuing to pray even when you cannot see how your request will unfold. It means believing that you can turn your longings into fulfilled du'a, even if the answer comes differently—or later—than expected.

## Yaqeen Vs. Self-Belief

While self-help teachings often say, "I create my reality," Islam reminds you: "Allah is the best of planners." Your role is one of effort—making du'a, taking practical steps, and maintaining your faith. The results, however, are ultimately in Allah's control.

This shift in perspective is liberating. You don't have to carry the burden of controlling outcomes. You have to show up with sincerity and trust that Allah is handling what you cannot.

## PROPHETIC STORIES OF YAQEEN

The prophets and righteous people throughout history demonstrate what yaqeen looks like in action:

- Ibrahim (AS): Thrown into the fire—Allah made it cool and safe
- Musa (AS): Trapped at sea—Allah parted the waters
- Maryam (AS): Alone in childbirth—Allah provided a miracle

These stories exemplify how yaqeen manifests in how you act when everything seems lost. True certainty influences your behavior: you trust, you endure, and you surrender to Allah's wisdom, even when circumstances look impossible.

## NURTURING YAQEEN THROUGH DAILY PRACTICES

Building and maintaining yaqeen isn't a one-time act; it's a continuous effort that requires daily discipline and mindfulness. By incorporating certain practices into your routine, you can deepen your trust in Allah and fortify your faith amid daily challenges. These small, consistent acts—when done with sincerity—serve as undeniable reminders of Allah's mercy, His Names, and His control over all matters.

- *Dhikr* (remembrance of Allah): Softens your heart and brings you closer to Allah. Regular remembrance creates a constant awareness of His presence.
- Qur'an: Strengthens trust and reassures you of Allah's mercy. When you read His words, they remind you of His promises and His care for His servants.

- Gratitude: Shifts your focus from lack to abundance, reinforcing your reliance on Allah's favors. When you remember what He's already given you, it becomes easier to trust Him with what you're still seeking.

These practices build strong yaqeen during peaceful times, but your faith will inevitably face challenges that test everything you've built.

## WHEN BELIEF IS TESTED

Shaytan will whisper, "It's not working." This is when your *yaqeen* is being tested. Remember, delay is not denial. Keep making du'a, and recall past moments when Allah answered you in better ways than you asked.

Doubt and despair are natural human emotions—but they're not places to dwell. When tested, return to dhikr, prayer, and trusted reminders of past answered du'as. Keep a journal of Allah's responses to your prayers—it becomes clear evidence during times of doubt.

> *"Call upon Allah while being certain of being answered."*
> (*Jami' at-Tirmidhi*, Book of Supplications, Hadith 3479)

> *"...for my Lord is (always) near, ready to answer."*
> (Qur'an 11:61)

But what happens when the test deepens, and you begin to wonder if Allah is responding at all?

## WHEN DU'A SEEMS UNANSWERED

Allah does not answer every du'a in the way or timeframe you expect. Not getting your du'a answered as expected isn't a sign that Allah has turned away. It's often a call to deeper trust and sometimes deeper spiritual work.

Some delays protect you from harm you can't see. Some redirections guide you toward something better. And sometimes, the silence is Allah holding you in a place of preparation, developing your character for what's coming.

Remember this meaningful hadith:

> *"A person's supplication will be accepted so long as he does not become impatient and say, 'I supplicated but it was not accepted.'"*
> (*Sahih Muslim*, Book of Dhikr, Hadith 2735,
> Also in: *Sahih al-Bukhari*, Book of Da'awat, Hadith 6340)

When your du'a seems unanswered, consider these possibilities:

- Reflect: Is Allah delaying to give you something better? Is this time of waiting developing patience, gratitude, or other spiritual qualities you I need?
- Renew: Continue asking with patience and sincerity. Sometimes, persistence itself is what Allah wants to see from you.
- Trust: Know that Allah's silence may be a form of mercy. What seems like "no" might be protection from something that would ultimately harm your spiritual growth.

Trust that Allah hears every sincere du'a —and responds to—in the way that is best for your *dunya* (this world) and *akhirah* (the next life).

Understanding these realities intellectually is one thing, but maintaining unwavering belief in the face of real challenges requires practical tools and daily discipline.

## How To Build Unshakeable Belief

Belief can be challenged by self-doubt, past disappointments, or other people's opinions—often unsolicited. When family members question your goals, when setbacks make you wonder if Allah is truly listening, or when your inner critic whispers that you're not worthy of what you're asking for, your yaqeen can waver.

The good news is that belief, like any spiritual muscle, can be strengthened through intentional practice. These practical methods strengthen yaqeen, drawn from both Islamic tradition and personal experience:

Daily Affirmation Practice

Instead of generic positive thinking, root your affirmations in Islamic truth:

- Manifesting-focused: "I am welcoming halal income into my life.
- Emotional grounding: "I am safe and guided by Allah's wisdom."
- Trust-based: "What Allah has written for me will reach me at the perfect time."

Inner Critic Exercise

When doubt creeps into your head, try this approach:

- Notice the voice: "I notice I'm telling myself this won't happen."
- Thank it for concern: "Thank you for trying to protect me from disappointment."
- Provide Islamic truth: "But Allah invites me to ask, and His mercy is greater than my fears."
- Redirect with du'a: "Ya Allah, help me trust Your love for me more than my fears about myself."

Belief Inventory Exercise

Think of your deepest du'a—the one that matters most to your heart. Now, honestly assess:

- What's your belief level? On a scale of 1-10, how strongly do you believe Allah will respond in a manner that is best for you?
- What story are you telling yourself? Are you focusing on Allah's generosity or your perceived unworthiness?

If you discover weak belief, don't judge yourself. Use it as information for where to focus your spiritual work.

## THE RELATIONSHIP BETWEEN BELIEF AND RECEIVING

Here's something crucial I've learned: Your capacity to believe you're worthy of receiving often limits your capacity to receive. Believing you are worthy isn't about deserving in a transactional sense—it's about truly understanding your position as Allah's beloved servant.

You need to believe:

- Allah wants good for you more than you want it for yourself
- Your du'as matter and are heard by the Creator of the universe
- You are worthy of Allah's mercy and blessings
- The delay isn't rejection—it's divine wisdom in action

When these beliefs become rooted in your heart, something shifts. You start asking with more confidence, working with more peace, and waiting with more serenity.

## HOW TO STRENGTHEN YAQEEN: PRACTICAL STEPS

Morning Practice: Begin each day by reciting Allah's names that relate to your current needs. If you're seeking provision, repeat "Ar-Razzaq" and reflect on its meaning.

Evening Reflection: Before sleep, remember three ways Allah showed His care for you that day, no matter how small.

Weekly Review: Look back at your du'a journal and note any patterns in how Allah has been responding to your prayers.

Monthly Gratitude: Write a letter to Allah expressing gratitude for both answered and "unanswered" prayers, acknowledging that His wisdom exceeds your understanding.

## SPIRITUAL TAKEAWAY

Faith isn't the absence of doubt but the decision to trust anyway. Yaqeen means walking with certainty, even when the path is unclear. It's not about seeing the destination but trusting the Guide who knows the way.

## JOURNEY PROMPTS

1. Describe a time when you held on to a belief despite uncertainty.
2. What helped you stay anchored?
3. What did Allah teach you through that experience?

## AS WE CONTINUE THE JOURNEY

You've learned to ask with sincerity and believe with yaqeen—unwavering certainty in Allah's response. Your heart is aligned, your trust is strong, and your du'a is clear.

But if you're like most people, you might be feeling a tension building: "I believe Allah will respond, but what am I supposed to do while I wait? Do I just sit here and pray?"

This tension is a sign of spiritual health—your soul recognizes that faith and action aren't opposites, they're partners. Islamic manifestation isn't about dreaming and waiting; it's about believing, praying, and moving with intention.

This foundation prepares you for what it means to "tie your camel" while maintaining complete *tawakkul* (trust and reliance on Allah) in Allah's plan, taking inspired action that honors both effort and surrender.

## DU'A

*Ya Allah, strengthen my faith and let my heart be firm in yaqeen. Help me trust Your love for me more than my fear of disappointment. Let my belief in Your goodness outweigh my doubts about myself."*

"And that there is nothing for man
except what he strives for."
(Qur'an 53:39)

# CHAPTER SEVEN
## STEP 4: ACTION WITH AMAL

You've learned to believe with *yaqeen* (certainty)—unwavering certainty in Allah's response. But manifestation in Islam isn't passive. It's not about dreaming and waiting—it's about believing, praying, and moving. Once you've clarified your intention, aligned it with divine values, and asked Allah with sincerity, the next step is to act. You don't fulfill faith through stillness alone—it requires motion.

## TIE YOUR CAMEL, AND TRUST IN ALLAH

One of the most well-known prophetic teachings perfectly captures the balance you need to strike. It comes from a hadith in *Tirmidhi*:

> A man said, *"O Messenger of Allah, should I tie my camel and trust in Allah, or should I leave her untied and trust in Allah?"* The Prophet (PBUH) replied: *"Tie her and trust in Allah."*
> (*Jami' at-Tirmidhi*, Book of Sifat al-Qiyamah, Hadith 2517)

This simple exchange teaches you a fundamental truth: *Tawakkul* (trust and reliance on Allah), which we will discuss in the next chapter... isn't the opposite of effort—it includes it. Placing trust in Allah means doing your part with complete reliance on the understanding that He controls the outcome. You secure your camel *and* trust Allah. You don't choose between action and trust—you embrace both.

## QUR'ANIC GUIDANCE ON TAKING ACTION

Change begins with action. One of my favorite sayings is "you can't just pray about it—you also have to be about it."

Islam teaches balance. We ask, we trust, and we act. Real tawakkul is not passive; it is the quiet strength of moving forward while trusting in the unseen. Du'a opens the gate, intention points the way—but action is how you walk through. Maryam (AS) was instructed by Allah, through divine inspiration, to shake the trunk of the palm tree during labor. (Qur'an 19:25-26) The prophets, who were also divinely guided, were people of tremendous action:

- *Prophet Nuh (AS)* built the ark (Qur'an 11:37-38)
- *Prophet Musa (AS)* struck the sea with his staff (Qur'an 26:63)
- And *Prophet Muhammad* (PBUH) migrated, negotiated treaties, led communities, and fought for justice—all while praying deeply and relying on Allah

This shows that even those with direct divine guidance still took concrete action as part of their trust in Allah. Islam doesn't ask you to sit back and wait. It invites you to partner your prayers with purposeful movement. The Qur'an makes this clear:

> *"Allah does not change a people's lot unless they change what is in their hearts."*
> (Qur'an 13:11)

You are part of the equation. You must match your internal transformation with external action.

## INSPIRED ACTION VS. DESPERATE HUSTLE

Here's something crucial I want you to understand: taking action doesn't mean frantic striving. Islamic action is intentional, ethical, and done with presence. It's infused with remembrance of Allah and guided by trust, not anxiety.

Inspired action feels different from desperate hustle:

- It may feel quiet and small, like writing the first page, sending the email, or registering for the class

- It's not always loud or flashy—it's often consistent, humble, and fueled by sincerity
- It comes from a place of trust rather than fear
- It includes regular pauses for prayer, reflection, and course correction

Desperate hustle, on the other hand:
- Comes from fear of not being enough or not doing enough
- Lacks spiritual grounding and often compromises values
- Focuses on speed over wisdom
- Exhausts rather than energizes

> *"It is part of the Mercy of Allah that thou dost deal gently with them Wert thou severe or harsh-hearted, they would have broken away from about thee: so pass over (Their faults), and ask for (Allah's) forgiveness for them; and consult them in affairs (of moment).*
> *Then, when thou hast Taken a decision trust in Allah. For Allah loves those who put their trust (in Him)."*
> (Qur'an 3:159)

The sequence is important: First, you reflect and seek guidance, then you decide, then you act, and finally, you trust. Action without reflection can lead you astray, but reflection without action keeps you stuck.

## WHAT DIVINELY ALIGNED ACTION LOOKS LIKE

When divine guidance aligns with your action:
- It feels sustainable: You can maintain this pace without burning out or compromising your spiritual practices.
- It honors your values: The means are as important as the ends— you won't compromise your integrity for faster results.
- It includes others: You consider how your actions affect your family, community, and the broader *ummah* (Muslim community).

- It makes space for Allah: You build in time for prayer, reflection, and course correction based on divine guidance.
- It feels peaceful: Even when challenging, there's an underlying sense that you're walking the right path.

## PRACTICAL STEPS FOR TAKING ALIGNED ACTION

### 1. Seek Allah's guidance through Istikhara

Before taking major action, turn to the prayer of Istikhara. This prayer isn't reserved only for life-changing decisions—you can seek divine guidance for smaller steps too. However, Istikhara works best when you've already done your homework: research your options, consult knowledgeable people, and think things through rationally. When you're still genuinely torn between choices despite this preparation, ask Allah to make the path clear if it's good for you and to close it if it's not. Remember, Istikhara complements your practical efforts—it doesn't replace them.

### 2. Break It Down

Large goals can feel overwhelming and lead to paralysis. Break your vision into smaller, manageable steps. Ask yourself: "What's one thing I can do this week that moves me closer to what I've been praying for?"

### 3. Take the Next Right Step

You don't need to see the whole staircase—just the next step. Focus on what's immediately in front of you rather than trying to control the entire journey.

### 4. Maintain Your Spiritual Practices

Don't let action become so consuming that you neglect prayer, Qur'an reading, or *dhikr* (remembrance of Allah). These practices keep you aligned and help you recognize when you're veering off course.

**5. Check Your Intentions Regularly**

Periodically ask yourself: "Am I doing this to serve Allah and fulfill my purpose, or am I being driven by ego, fear, or the desire to impress others?"

## WHEN YOU'RE AFRAID

Fear is natural when you're stepping into the unknown. Your job isn't to control the outcome—your job is to take the step.

> *"Strive for that which will benefit you,*
> *seek the help of Allah, and do not feel helpless."*
> (*Sahih Muslim*, Book of Destiny, Hadith 2664)

When fear arises, try this approach:

- Acknowledge it: "I notice I'm feeling afraid about this step."
- Ask why: "What specifically am I afraid of? Is this fear protecting me from real danger, or is it just resistance to growth?"
- Pray about it: "Ya Allah, if this step is good for me, give me courage. If it's not, redirect me to what's better."
- Take the step anyway: "I'll move forward with trust, knowing You're with me."

Passivity in the name of "trust" isn't tawakkul—it's *tawaakul* (false reliance). Islam teaches us to hope with effort, trust with planning, and have faith with movement.

## THE BALANCE OF EFFORT AND SURRENDER

Action completes the cycle of belief. When you act, even in uncertainty, you declare with your limbs what your heart believes: Allah is in control, but I will show up.

As Islamic wisdom teaches: 'Work for your worldly life as if you will live forever, and work for your afterlife as if you will die tomorrow. This means, you put in the full effort while maintaining perspective. You plan as if the outcome depends on you, but you trust as if it depends entirely on Allah—because it does.

## RECOGNIZING DIVINE SUPPORT IN YOUR ACTIONS

As you begin taking aligned action, watch for signs that Allah is supporting your efforts:

- **Doors opening:** Opportunities appearing that you didn't create.
- **Ease in difficulty:** Challenges that resolve more smoothly than expected.
- **Right people appearing:** Meeting individuals who can help or guide you.
- **Inner peace:** Feeling calm even when circumstances are uncertain.
- **Increased** *barakah (blessing)*: Experiencing blessing and multiplication in your efforts.

These aren't guarantees that everything will go according to your plan, but they're often signs that you're walking a path that has divine approval.

## WHEN ACTION FEELS OVERWHELMING

Sometimes, you may feel like you're not doing enough, or that others are moving faster toward their goals. Remember:

- **Your timeline is unique:** Allah's timing for you is different from His timing for others.
- **Consistency matters more than intensity:** Small, steady steps often accomplish more than sporadic bursts of activity.
- **Quality over quantity:** One aligned action is worth more than ten scattered efforts.
- **Trust the process:** Your job is to show up; Allah's job is to orchestrate the outcome.

# REAL STORY OF TAKING ACTION ON MY LAST BOOK

The principle of aligned action transformed how I wrote *Crescent Over Crossroads*. For years, I carried this vision in my heart—a desire to tell my story as an African American Muslim woman in America. I wanted to reflect on my journey to and through Islam, the challenges of navigating identity, and the process of becoming my most authentic self. I felt called to merge my legal background, my work in diversity and inclusion, and the lived wisdom of a life filled with faith, struggle, and transformation.

But I kept putting it off, waiting for perfect conditions—more time, more qualifications, more research. In truth, I was procrastinating, disguising my fear as preparation. I even questioned what impact it may have on my business – telling the story of a African American Muslim. The breakthrough came through divine intervention: my Arabic and Qur'an teacher lovingly challenged me to finish the book by year's end, with just thirty days left. That moment became a turning point. I stopped hesitating. I surrendered my doubts. I walked toward Allah, and He ran toward me.

I didn't have a grand writing retreat or a perfect schedule. I started by writing each chapter separately. I wrote from the heart. I made du'a for clarity and usefulness. And piece by piece, the book took form.

What looked like a sudden achievement to others was actually created through small, faithful steps—consistent effort aligned with sincere intention, paired with tawakkul. That's what aligned action looks like: doing your part while relying on Allah for the outcome. When you stop waiting for perfect conditions and start walking toward Allah, He runs toward you.

## A NOTE ON PERFECTIONISM

Here's a little aside and hopefully a lot of encouragement: Stop waiting for perfection. This is not the perfect realm. We are not perfect, and we will not produce perfect things. Even large companies like Apple release a product, discover an issue, and then release an update to fix the bug.

Your action doesn't need to be flawless—it needs to be faithful. Start with sincere intention, do your best with the knowledge and resources you have today, and trust that Allah will guide your course corrections along the way. *Tawakkul* includes the understanding that growth happens through iteration, not through waiting until you have everything figured out.

Move forward with what you have, where you are, trusting that Allah will make your path clear as you walk it.

## SPIRITUAL TAKEAWAY

Faith without action is incomplete, but action without faith is exhausting. When you combine sincere effort with complete trust in Allah's plan, you step into the sacred space of Islamic manifestation—working as if everything depends on you while knowing that everything depends on Him.

---

## JOURNEY PROMPTS

1. Where have you been waiting for perfect conditions instead of taking the next right step?

2. What's the difference between *tawakkul* (trust in Allah) and *tawakul* (false passivity) in your current situation?

3. Write an action plan for one of your major goals, breaking it into monthly, weekly, and daily steps. Include prayer checkpoints.

4. This week, take one meaningful action toward your goal each day, preceded by "*Bismillah*" (In the name of Allah) and followed by "*Alhamdulillah*" (all praise is to Allah).

---

## AS WE CONTINUE THE JOURNEY

We are moving along. You are taking aligned action while maintaining trust in Allah's plan, working as if everything depended on you while knowing that everything depended on Him. This balance is beautiful in theory, but in practice, it often leads to the true test of the manifestation journey - waiting.

You've clarified your intention. You've made sincere du'a. You've taken meaningful action. And now... you wait.

This waiting period tests everything you've learned. It's where many people lose faith, become anxious, or try to force outcomes. But what if I told you that this space between action and result is the most spiritually fertile ground in your entire journey?

Building on this understanding, we'll explore how to master this waiting period through two essential spiritual states: unwavering trust in Allah's plan and graceful surrender to His timing.

## DU'A

*"Ya Allah, guide my steps and bless my efforts. Help me take action from a place of trust rather than fear. Make my work a form of worship and let every step draw me closer to You and to the purpose You've written for me."*

"Whoever submits
his whole self to Allah,
and is a doer of good,
has grasped indeed
the most trustworthy hand-hold:
and with Allah rests the End and
Decision of (all) affairs"
(Qur'an 31:22)

# CHAPTER EIGHT
## STEPS 5 & 6: TRUST WITH TAWAKKUL & SURRENDER WITH RIDA

You've learned to take aligned action while maintaining faith in Allah's plan. Now comes perhaps the deepest spiritual work of your manifestation journey: learning to trust the process completely and surrendering your attachment to specific outcomes. These two spiritual states work together—trust propels you forward, while surrender allows you to rest in Allah's wisdom.

## STEP 5: TRUST - WALKING FORWARD WITH TAWAKKUL

### Embracing Tawakkul

Trust is that delicate moment when you've done everything you can, and now you need to let Allah take over. It's not giving up—it's recognizing where your effort ends and His plan begins. Acting with intention, prayer, and trust is how you move from supplication to transformation. But don't confuse *tawakkul* (trust and reliance on Allah) with passivity. Aligned action is movement inspired by faith, not fear.

Ask yourself these questions to gauge your level of trust:

- Does this choice bring you peace?
- Is it in line with who you are becoming?
- Can you pursue it while maintaining your spiritual practices?

Tawakkul is walking toward your goals with trust in your heart. If belief is the seed, then trust is the soil in which you must plant it.

Tawakkul is sincere reliance on Allah after making your effort. It's not passivity, and it's not blind optimism. It's the active state of placing your heart in Allah's hands while your feet keep moving toward your goals.

> *"If you were to rely upon Allah with the reliance He is due, you would be provided for like the birds: they leave in the morning with empty stomachs and return full by dusk."*
> (*Jami' at-Tirmidhi*, Book of Zuhd, Hadith 2344)

The bird doesn't sit in its nest, waiting for food to fall. It flies. It searches. It works. And it trusts. That's tawakkul—the perfect balance of effort and surrender.

Tawakkul vs. Tawaakul

Understanding this distinction is crucial for your spiritual development:

- Tawakkul: Trusting Allah after effort → Peace and spiritual maturity
- Tawaakul: Claiming to trust Allah without effort → Inaction and unmet expectations

True tawakkul requires you to show up fully, then release the outcome completely.

A Living Example: Hajar's Tawakkul

When Allah commanded Ibrahim (AS) to leave Hajar (AS) in the barren desert with her infant son, she ran between the hills of Safa and Marwah—seven times—not knowing where help would come from. She didn't sit still and wait for a miracle. And it was in that moment of movement, born from complete trust, that Allah caused the well of Zamzam to spring forth.

Tawakkul isn't about waiting in the dark for the light to come. It's about walking with faith through the dark, knowing Allah is the light guiding your steps.

Trusting When You Can't See the Whole Path

Tawakkul isn't just believing something will happen—it's believing that even if it doesn't happen the way you imagined, Allah's plan is still better. It's walking forward without needing to see the whole path, knowing that the One who paved it is with you.

> *"Whoever submits his whole self to Allah, and is a doer of good, has grasped indeed the most trustworthy hand-hold: and with Allah rests the End and Decision of (all) affairs."*
> (Qur'an 31:22)

*Du'a* (supplication) for Trust: *"O Allah, place trust in my heart for Your plan, even when I cannot see it. Strengthen my steps, calm my fears, and help me walk forward with reliance on You."*

Take the step, even if it's small, even if your heart trembles, because tawakkul doesn't wait. It moves. It trusts. And it grows.

## STEP 6: SURRENDER - LETTING GO WITH RIDA AND SABR

Once you've asked, moved, believed and trusted, the next step is letting go of the "how" and "when." You keep showing up and doing your part, but your heart lets go of the outcome—because your trust is in Allah, not in your plan.

Your heart letting go of the "how" and "when" and trusting in Allah is the sacred art of surrender—the final release of control and the deepest form of faith. Surrender isn't weakness. It's the deepest strength—one born of humility, faith, and complete awareness that Allah knows what you do not. It's the art of letting go, not because you no longer care, but because you care enough to stop clinging and start trusting.

The Sacred Release Through Rida and Sabr

This sacred release is practiced through two spiritual states:

- Rida: Contentment with what Allah has willed

- Sabr: Patient endurance while waiting for what may still come

Together, they allow you to breathe deeply, even when the future feels uncertain.

> *"No kind of calamity can occur, except by the leave of Allah: and if anyone believes in Allah, (Allah) guides his heart (aright): for Allah knows all things."*
> (Qur'an 64:11)

This verse anchors us in trust, even when life feels uncertain. It reassures us that belief itself is a guidance system—one that can carry us through any trial, if our hearts remain open to Allah's wisdom.

The Beauty of Letting Go

Letting go doesn't mean giving up; it means releasing control. It means laying down the burden of control—the weight of needing things to happen your way, in your time. It's trusting that if something were meant for you, it would not pass you by. And if it passed you by, it was never written for you.

The Qur'an gently reminds you:

> *"But it is possible that ye dislike a thing which is good for you; and that ye love a thing which is bad for you. But Allah knoweth, and ye know not"*
> (Qur'an 2:216)

Letting go isn't the absence of care. It's the presence of peace. When you surrender to Allah's *qadr* (divine decree), you're not abandoning your hopes. You're opening your heart to something more expansive— trusting that Allah's plan holds more wisdom than your limited vision can perceive.

Surrender vs. Letting Go

There's a subtle but beautiful distinction between these two concepts:

- Surrender (Rida - Contentment with Allah's decree) is what happens in your heart. It's a softening toward Allah's will. It says, "Even if I don't get what I want, I trust that You know best and I am content." "Even if it takes longer, I am patient." "Even if I don't understand, I trust."

- Letting Go (Sabr/Patience) is what happens in your body and mind. It's the release of obsessive thinking, the refusal to panic, the redirection of energy toward things within your control.

Both require deep emotional strength—and spiritual softness. Letting go doesn't make you weak; it makes you strong. It shows that you trust the One who is strong enough to carry what you can't.

Signs You Haven't Let Go

Sometimes, you say you've surrendered—but your actions tell another story. Look for these signs that your heart is still holding on too tightly:

- Constantly checking your phone or email for updates
- Feeling anxious, irritable, or distracted about the outcome
- Comparing yourself to others who've "manifested" what you want
- Resenting the delay or doubting your du'a

These aren't signs of failure but invitations. Invitations to come back to *sabr* (Patience), to *ridaI* (Contentment), and to re-center your trust.

Redirecting Your Focus

Letting go doesn't mean you sit and wait. It means you move forward in other ways. Shift your energy toward:

- Other joyful, meaningful goals
- Acts of service or generosity
- Deepening worship and *dhikr* (remembrance of Allah)
- Spending time with family or in nature
- Developing hobbies or creative outlets

Sometimes, the blessing doesn't arrive until you're no longer watching the door so intently.

## REAL STORY OF DIVINE ORCHESTRATION THROUGH SERVICE

For years, I had dreamed of living in a Muslim country for at least one year—specifically Morocco. I visualized it, added it to my vision board, and prayed about it constantly. I didn't know how I was going to finance such an experience, but I continued to make du'a about it, trusting that if Allah willed it, He would make a way.

The door began to open in an unexpected place. While serving on a board, our organization planned its annual conference during Ramadan. As the only Muslim on the board, I insisted we reserve a room for salah at the convention center, even though it would add to the budget. I faced pushback, but I held firm. When they agreed, they wanted to open the room to everyone by labeling it a "quiet room," but I stood my ground—it had to be a salah hall. At a conference of nearly 1,000 people, there were only 3 Muslims that I know of.

The first blessing: As a result of that decision, I met a sister from Abu Dhabi who had come to the conference and was grateful to find a place to pray. I introduced myself and invited her to join me for *Tarawih* (voluntary prayers performed during the nights of Ramadan), and we formed an instant bond. Before the conference ended, she invited me to come visit her in the UAE. About four months later, I was on a plane heading to Abu Dhabi. That moment began a beautiful sisterhood that continues today. This was my first trip to a Muslim country.

The cascade of new blessings: That first trip to the UAE opened doors I never anticipated. My new sister and I later traveled together to Uzbekistan. She was instrumental in me traveling to Jordan and making my first journey to Mecca for Umrah. Each journey built my confidence and familiarity with Muslim countries.

The culminating blessing: Eventually, I visited Morocco on what was meant to be a recharge trip while grieving my mother's loss. While there—in a state of complete surrender and healing—I secured a major contract after not working for an extended period. It was that contract that made it possible for me to move to Morocco for two years, fulfilling the exact dream I had been praying for.

What started with insisting on one prayer room during Ramadan for just 3 Muslims at a 1,000-person conference became a chain of divine provision that took me around the Muslim world, brought me a sister for life, sustained me through grief, and ultimately led to living my dream of residing in Morocco. *Subhan'Allah*—when you make space for Allah in your decisions, He makes space for you in His plans.

This experience taught me that *rida* and *sabr* aren't passive states—they're dynamic forces of alignment. When you let go of how it must happen and stay faithful to who you're asking, the outcome may exceed even your most carefully laid plans.

Letting go isn't laziness. It's spiritual maturity. It's choosing serenity over striving, peace over panic, and divine wisdom over self-will. You won't always get what you want. But when you walk the path with rida and sabr, you'll always be where you need to be. And that is more than enough.

> *"Amazing is the affair of the believer. Verily, all of his affairs are good. If something good happens, he is grateful, and that is good for him. If something bad happens, he is patient, and that is good for him."*
> (*Sahih Muslim*, Book of Zuhd, Hadith 2999)

But what about those times when Allah's response feels absent altogether? When weeks, months, or even years pass without the breakthrough you've been seeking?

## WHEN DU'AS ARE DELAYED

Sometimes, what you think is a delay is actually:

- A redirection toward something better
- A form of protection from harm you can't see
- An opportunity to deepen your reliance on Allah
- A test of your patience and spiritual maturity

Surrender helps you release the need to rush and instead find rest in divine timing.

The beautiful paradox of Islamic manifestation is this: the moment you stop frantically chasing your du'a and start walking peacefully toward Allah, you often find that what you were seeking was walking toward you all along. Trust the process, surrender the timeline, and let Allah's perfect wisdom unfold in your life.

## SPIRITUAL TAKEAWAY

Tawakkul isn't passive—it's walking forward with your heart in Allah's hands, even when you can't see the finish line. True surrender isn't resignation but serenity in Allah's decree. When you walk the path of both action and trust, peace and progress naturally coexist.

---

## JOURNEY PROMPTS

1. How confident are you that Allah hears your du'a, even if the response doesn't come in the way or timing you expect? What helps you stay spiritually grounded in the waiting?
2. What past experience shook your trust in du'a, and what would it take to heal that wound?
3. Describe a situation where surrendering control led to a better outcome than you could have planned. How does this experience strengthen your tawakkul?

4. This week, practice this daily affirmation after *Fajr* (dawn prayer): "Allah hears my du'a, sees my effort, and will respond in the way that's best for me."

## AS WE CONTINUE THE JOURNEY

You've learned to trust the process entirely and surrender your attachment to specific outcomes. This surrender isn't giving up—it's the deepest form of faith, allowing your heart to rest in Allah's wisdom even when the path isn't clear.

But surrender leads to something even more beautiful: the ability to recognize and receive Allah's response with the grace and awareness it deserves. Most people focus so intensely on asking that they miss the subtle ways Allah begins to answer. When you've done the work, asked with sincerity, believed with yaqeen, acted with purpose, and surrendered with grace, you enter a sacred space of receptivity. In our final step, we'll explore how to receive Allah's blessings with the gratitude and presence that invites even more divine favor into your life.

## DU'A

*"Ya Allah, teach me to trust You completely. Help me release control and find peace in Your timing. Grant me rida and sabr. Help me release what I cannot control, and fill my heart with peace in what You have written for me."*

"And remember! your Lord caused to be declared (publicly): 'If ye are grateful, I will add more (favours) unto you; But if ye show ingratitude, truly My punishment is terrible indeed.'"
(Qur'an 14:7)

# CHAPTER NINE
## STEP 7: RECEIVE WITH SHUKR

You've learned to surrender with *rida* (contentment) and wait with *Sabr* (patience). Now comes the culminating experience of your manifestation journey: receiving Allah's response with gratitude and grace. Receiving is more than just getting—it's a spiritual state of readiness, awareness, and humble recognition of Allah's generosity in your life.

> *"If ye are grateful, I will add more (favours) unto you"*
> (Qur'an 14:7)

Often, after releasing your du'a in surrender, signs begin to appear: a phone call, an opportunity, an inner nudge, a door opening where you didn't expect one. The key is to stay spiritually awake and recognize these moments. Receiving requires humility, clarity, and, above all, *shukr*—deep gratitude to the One who provides.

## THE ISLAMIC UNDERSTANDING OF ABUNDANCE

The Law of Attraction teaches that our thoughts, feelings, and energy shape our experiences. At its core, this idea resonates with a deeply rooted truth that already exists within Islam: gratitude attracts more blessings.

In *The Magic*, Rhonda Byrne quotes the Qur'an Surah 14, verse 7:

"And (remember) when God proclaimed: 'If you are grateful, I will give you more; but if you are ungrateful verily my punishment is indeed severe.'"

This universal principle—that gratitude brings increase—finds its clearest and most sacred expression in the Qur'an itself. Allah tells you that gratitude (*shukr*) isn't just a feeling but a spiritual force that unlocks more - more provision, more ease, more *barakah* (blessing). It's not simply a mindset; it's a form of *ibadah* (worship).

While the Law of Attraction describes gratitude as a kind of energetic magnet, you, as a Muslim, understand it as a key to divine generosity. Allah is *Al-Karim* (The Most Generous) and *Ash-Shakoor* (The Most Appreciative). He not only appreciates your gratitude, but He multiplies your reward for it.

Where some may speak of the universe responding to vibrations, you know it's Allah who responds to sincerity. Gratitude is a magnet, yes—but it draws blessings because Allah has promised it will.

Gratitude (*shukr*) isn't just a positive mindset—it's a form of worship. Your tradition even gives you a physical expression of gratitude: *Sujud ash-Shukr* (the Prostration of Gratitude). In moments of deep thankfulness, as Muslims, we learn to fall into prostration—not just as part of prayer but as a spontaneous act of honoring the One who gives.

> *"The closest that a servant comes to his Lord is when he is prostrating, so make plenty of supplication then."*
> (*Sahih Muslim*, He Book of Prayer,
> Hadith 482 Narrated by Abu Huraira (RA))

*Sujud* (prostration) isn't only an expression of humility—it's also one of the most spiritually connecting postures for *du'a* (supplication). Whether it's gratitude for what you've received or longing for what you're seeking, let your du'a rise from the lowest position of your body, and watch how Allah elevates you.

## THE THREE DIMENSIONS OF GRATITUDE: IMAM AL-GHAZALI'S TIMELESS WISDOM

In Islam, gratitude—*shukr*—is far more than a polite expression or a passing emotion. It's a way of living that engages your heart, your tongue, and your body in acknowledgment of Allah's boundless mercy. One of the most beautiful frameworks for understanding gratitude comes from

Imam Abu Hamid al-Ghazali (1058-1111 CE), a towering figure in Islamic scholarship known for harmonizing outward practice with inner spirituality.

Imam Al-Ghazali was a jurist, theologian, and mystic whose writings continue to have a significant influence to this day. Born in present-day Iran, he authored the renowned *Ihya 'Ulum al-Din* (The Revival of the Religious Sciences), a work that continues to shape how Muslims around the world understand the relationship between faith, practice, and the soul.

Al-Ghazali taught that genuine gratitude manifests in three interrelated forms, each reflecting a deeper level of awareness and worship.

## 1. Gratitude of the Heart (Shukr bi'l-Qalb)

This is the inward, contemplative awareness that all blessings—seen and unseen—come from Allah. It's the quiet recognition that every breath, every bite, every ease after difficulty is a divine gift.

To cultivate this form of gratitude, spend time in *tafakkur* (Contemplation) —reflecting deeply on the blessings in your life. Tafakkur might look like sitting in silence, journaling your thoughts, or simply closing your eyes and recalling the mercies you often overlook. Even the ability to reflect is a mercy.

> *"And ye have no good thing but is from Allah"*
> (Qur'an 16:53)

## 2. Gratitude of the Tongue (Shukr bi'l-Lisan)

The next level of gratitude is verbal. It's when your heart's awareness finds expression through your tongue—through *dhikr* (remembrance of Allah), du'a, and words of praise.

Saying "*Alhamdulillah*" (all praise is due to Allah), isn't just a reflex— it's a declaration of your relationship with the Giver. It's an act of worship that transforms ordinary moments into sacred ones. Make it a habit to speak your gratitude aloud during your du'a journaling. Name your blessings. Thank Allah directly.

> *"Allah is pleased with the servant who, when he eats something, praises Him, and when he drinks something, praises Him."*
> (*Sahih Muslim*, The Book of Drinks,
> Hadith 2734, Narrated by Anas ibn Malik (RA))

3. Gratitude of the Body and Limbs (Shukr bi'l-Badan wa'l-Arkan)

This is the most complete form of gratitude: to show your thanks through action. When your limbs obey Allah, you spend time in service, and you use your body in ways that are pleasing to Him—that is *shukr* in motion.

It's in the way you pray with presence. In the way you serve others and in how you walk away from what displeases Allah, even when no one is watching.

And sometimes, it's in how you fall to the ground in *Sujud ash-Shukr*—the prostration of gratitude—when words fail, and your body becomes the only appropriate response to the magnitude of Allah's mercy.

Gratitude in Islam is holistic. It begins in your heart, moves to your tongue, and completes in your body. Imam Al-Ghazali's model reminds you that *shukr* isn't simply something you feel—it's something you live.

When practiced in all its dimensions, gratitude becomes a powerful form of worship that invites more blessings, deepens trust in Allah, and anchors your soul in contentment. As mentioned earlier in this chapter, the Qur'an promises:

> *"If ye are grateful, I will add more (favours) unto you"*
> (Qur'an 14:7)

This verse bears repeating because gratitude is so important to fulfillment of dreams. When practiced in all its dimensions, gratitude becomes a powerful form of worship that invites more blessings, deepens trust in Allah, and anchors your soul in contentment.

## RECEIVING WITH SPIRITUAL AWARENESS

Receiving with gratitude completes the spiritual cycle of du'a. It reflects the patience (*sabr*) and contentment (*rida*) you've already cultivated—but with an open heart ready to embrace what has arrived.

Receiving begins not with what's in your hands but with what's in your heart. If your rigid expectations or impatience cloud your heart, you may overlook the blessing that has already arrived.

Receiving is about shukr—gratitude in action. It's also about humility and preparedness. It's about living as though Allah has already answered your du'a and trusting that what is arriving is precisely what you need.

## REAL STORY OF RECEIVING WITH SHUKR

Allah has shown me His provision in unexpected ways many times over. This moment especially moved me.

I recall a period when I was intensely focused on making money, to the point where it began to cloud my judgment. I told myself I was budgeting, being responsible, but underneath that was a feeling of lack. I had planned to skip my usual Sunday brunch at my favorite restaurant to save money.

But something in me shifted. I reminded myself: don't give in to the feeling of scarcity. Don't shrink your life out of fear. I chose to go anyway—not in recklessness, but in quiet trust that Allah is the Provider.

As I sat enjoying my meal, a man I had never met before walked by my table. Without saying much, he put money down to pay for my brunch. All he said was that he was moved to do that. That moment stunned me. It was a divine reminder: when you trust in Allah, blessings arrive from sources you could never have imagined. It also taught me this—sometimes it's not about money at all. If Allah blesses you directly with the experience or ease you were trying to buy, the money becomes irrelevant.

Provision doesn't always look like a paycheck. Sometimes, it's a moment of barakah delivered through the hands of a stranger—at precisely the right time.

This experience reminded me that receiving requires spiritual awareness. I could have dismissed this as a "coincidence" or focused on feeling embarrassed about accepting help from a stranger. Instead, I chose to receive it as a sign of Allah's care and a reminder that provision comes from sources you never could have planned or predicted.

## PRACTICAL GRATITUDE PRACTICES

### Daily Gratitude Ritual

Morning Practice: Before you ask Allah for anything new, spend five minutes thanking Him for three specific blessings from the previous day. Evening Reflection: End your day by writing down three ways Allah showed His care for you, no matter how small.

### Answered Du'a Journal

Keep a record of:

- Du'as that Allah answered exactly as requested
- Du'as that Allah answered differently but better than expected
- Du'as that seemed as if Allah didn't answer but led to unexpected blessings
- Times when "no" turned out to be protection

This journal becomes undeniable evidence of Allah's responsiveness during times of doubt.

### Gratitude in Action

- Share the blessing: When you receive something you prayed for, find a way to help someone else receive something similar.
- Increased charity: Let gratitude flow into increased *sadaqah* (voluntary charity) and service to others.

- Community celebration: Share appropriate good news with family and friends, always attributing success to Allah.

## SPIRITUAL TAKEAWAY

Gratitude is more than a feeling—it's a spiritual frequency that opens your heart to receive more from Allah. When you thank Him, you're not just acknowledging past blessings; you're preparing your heart to recognize and receive future ones. *Shukr* completes the cycle of manifestation by transforming receiving into a form of worship.

## JOURNEY PROMPTS

1. How do you typically respond when Allah answers your du'a—with entitled expectation or humble gratitude?
2. What blessings in your life have you started taking for granted that once were earnest du'as?
3. Write about a time when receiving what you wanted required you to grow into someone ready to handle it. What did you learn?
4. This week, start a gratitude journal specifically for answered du'as, both recent and past. Add one entry each night.

## AS WE CONTINUE THE JOURNEY

You've now learned the complete seven-step framework of Islamic manifestation. From visualization with *niyyah* (intention) to receiving with shukr, you have the spiritual technology to align your dreams with divine will. But frameworks are only as powerful as the integrity with which one applies them.

As you begin living these principles, you'll face tests that textbooks can't prepare you for. The next phase of your journey isn't about learning new concepts—it's about becoming someone who can live these principles with unshakeable integrity, even when it costs you. Let's explore how to manifest with Allah truly at the center, not just in your words, but in every decision you make.

# DU'A

*"Ya Allah, make me among the grateful. Let my heart recognize Your gifts, both large and small. Help my actions reflect Your praise, and make my gratitude a source of increased blessings for myself and my community."*

"Do ye enjoin right conduct on the people, and forget (to practise it) yourselves, and yet ye study the Scripture? Will ye not understand?" (Qur'an 2:44)

# INTERLUDE
## FROM KNOWING TO LIVING

You've journeyed through the heart of the framework—seven steps rooted in sacred guidance that align your dreams with divine will.

You've learned to visualize with pure *niyyah* (intention), clarifying what your heart truly seeks. You've discovered how to ask Allah with focused du'a that cuts through spiritual noise. You've built *yaqeen* (certainty)—an unshakeable belief that transforms hope into certainty. You've taken aligned action that honors both effort and trust. You've practiced *tawakkul* (trust and reliance on Allah)—walking forward even when the path isn't fully visible. You've explored surrender—releasing control while deepening faith. And you've opened yourself to receive with grateful recognition of Allah's perfect timing.

But if you're like most readers at this point, you may feel both inspired and overwhelmed. You understand the principles intellectually, but there's a gap—a bridge you need to cross between knowledge and lived experience.

Maybe you're wondering:

- "How do I actually live this when my family doesn't understand?"
- "What happens when I face real ethical dilemmas at work?"
- "How do I maintain this spiritual alignment during difficult seasons?"
- "What if I start well but lose momentum after a few weeks?"

These questions aren't obstacles—they're invitations. They're your soul asking not just to learn about Islamic manifestation, but to become someone who naturally embodies these principles.

## FROM INSPIRATION TO TRANSFORMATION

Here's what I've learned from my journey and from working with others: Information without application is just inspiration that fades.

You can read about tawakkul a hundred times, but until you practice it during a job interview that determines your family's financial future, it remains theoretical. You can understand sabr intellectually, but until you exercise patience while waiting for Allah's response to your most heartfelt du'a, it's just a beautiful concept.

The difference between those who transform their lives and those who collect spiritual knowledge lies in sustained, authentic, integrity-rooted implementation.

## WHAT PART III WILL GIVE YOU

Part III isn't about learning new concepts. You have the framework. Now, we're going to make it unshakeable.

In the upcoming chapters, you'll discover:

- How to maintain integrity when it costs you (Chapter 10) - What happens when the promotion you've been making du'a for requires compromising your values? How do you navigate the gray areas where Islamic guidance meets modern dilemmas?

- How to clear the internal blocks that sabotage your progress (Chapter 11) - Why do some people seem effortlessly aligned while others struggle despite their sincerity? We'll identify and start to heal the hidden wounds that create resistance to receiving Allah's blessings.

- How to create daily practices that sustain your spiritual alignment (Chapter 12) - You've learned the seven-step framework, but how do you maintain that spiritual connection day after day? Not overwhelming routines that you'll abandon in two weeks, but simple, powerful practices that become as natural as breathing and keep you anchored in divine purpose through busy schedules, life changes, and inevitable distractions.

- How to create a vision board with *taqwa* (God-consciousness) (Chapter 13) - You've learned the framework, but how do you give your du'as visual form without falling into manifestation culture's pitfalls? We'll explore how to create a tactile representation of your prayers that keeps Allah at the center, deepens your spiritual focus, and serves as a daily reminder of your sacred intentions rather than a magical wish list.

- How to apply these principles through every season of life (Chapter 14) - From career transitions to family changes, from health challenges to financial struggles—your framework will adapt and strengthen.

- How to build community that supports your journey (Chapter 15) - Because walking this path alone can be harder than walking with others, and Allah has placed certain people in your life for your mutual elevation.

## WHERE THE JOURNEY DEEPENS

The actual test isn't whether you can make du'a in a peaceful masjid—it's whether you can maintain tawakkul in a chaotic workplace.

The genuine challenge isn't whether you can feel grateful when everything goes right—it's whether you can practice shukr when Allah's response looks different from what you expected.

What truly tests you isn't whether you can visualize your dreams in solitude—it's whether you can hold your vision with sabr when others question your path.

This is where theory meets reality, where principles become practice, and where your spiritual knowledge transforms into lived truth.

## Your Invitation Forward

The foundation is set. Your heart is prepared. Now, let's discover how to live these principles with integrity and consistency, no matter what circumstances you face.

Part III will give you the practical tools to navigate real-world challenges while maintaining your spiritual center, create sustainable daily practices, and build the community support that sustains your journey through every season of life.

*Bismillah* (In the name of Allah). Let's continue this journey together—not just as seekers of blessings but as servants growing closer to the One who blesses.

# PART THREE
## APPLIED
## MANIFESTATION
## IN A MUSLIM'S LIFE

*"O ye who believe! Stand out firmly for justice, as witnesses to Allah, even as against yourselves, or your parents, or your kin."*
(Qur'an 4:135)

"But seek, with the (wealth) which Allah has bestowed on thee, the Home of the Hereafter, nor forget thy portion in this world..."
(Qur'an 28:77)

# CHAPTER TEN
## MANIFESTING WITH INTEGRITY AND ALLAH AT THE CENTER

You began this journey wanting to bring your dreams to life. But you've probably uncovered something deeper—this isn't just about attracting blessings. It's about becoming someone ready to receive them with grace, clarity, and surrender to Allah's will.

Sometimes we pray with all our heart for something, and Allah grants it—only for us to realize later that it was never what we truly needed. It reminds me of the saying, " *We spend our whole lives climbing the ladder of success, only to realize it's been leaning against the wrong wall.* " (Stephen R. Covey, *The 7 Habits of Highly Effective People*, 1989)

In other words, we can be persistent, strategic, and even prayerful—but if our vision isn't grounded in divine wisdom, we may find ourselves asking for what dazzles the ego rather than what nourishes the soul. Sometimes the gift is not in the attainment, but in the disillusionment that brings us closer to clarity—and ultimately, closer to Allah.

## REMEMBERING THE SOURCE OF ALL BLESSINGS

There's an old joke that never gets old—probably because it's so true. A man is driving around the parking lot of a busy shopping center, circling and circling like he's doing tawaf around the mall. He's getting desperate. He finally raises his hands and says, *"Ya Allah, please! If You help me find a parking space, I swear I'll start praying on time, give more in sadaqah, and get to Jumu'ah before the Imam!"*

Just then, right in front of him—a car pulls out and a spot opens up. He slams the brakes, pulls in fast and says, *"Never mind, God. I found one!"*

We laugh, but don't we do the same thing? We cry, we beg, we negotiate with Allah when we want something. But the moment the ease comes, we act like it was all us. Like we manifested it, masterminded it, or maneuvered it—but we forget that we made *du'a* (supplication) for it 27 times last week.

Let's be honest: sometimes we treat divine help like customer service—we only remember it when something goes wrong. But Allah says:

> *'And ye have no good thing but is from Allah'*
> (Qur'an 16:53)

So even when the parking space opens up, don't forget who moved the car. This light-hearted reminder points to a deeper truth: maintaining awareness of Allah's role in all our successes requires constant mindfulness and intentional practice.

## WHAT DOES INTEGRITY LOOK LIKE IN PRACTICE?

To manifest with integrity means to seek from Allah that which is halal (permissible) and to do so with sincerity, righteousness, and ethical alignment. In Islam, integrity isn't only about being honest and just with others—it's about being truthful with yourself and, most importantly, with Allah.

> *"Allah commands justice, the doing of good, and liberality*
> *to kith and kin, and He forbids all shameful deeds, and*
> *injustice and rebellion: He instructs you, that ye may*
> *receive admonition."*
> (Qur'an 16:90)

While these principles are clear in theory, real-life situations often present complex choices where the "right" path isn't immediately obvious. How do you maintain integrity when faced with competing priorities, family pressure, or financial stress?

# INTEGRITY DILEMMAS: NAVIGATING DIFFICULT CHOICES

The following scenarios are fictional, but they reflect the kinds of choices many of us face. Use them as a framework for thinking through your own integrity decisions.

## SCENARIO 1: THE CAREER CROSSROADS

The Situation: You've been praying for a promotion for months. When the opportunity finally comes, you discover that the company may ask you manage campaigns that use misleading claims to sell products. The salary increase would solve your family's financial stress, but the role conflicts with your values.

Heart-Check Questions:
- Would I feel peaceful explaining this job to Allah in my du'a?
- Could I use this position to create positive change from within, in other words, would I have the power to change the campaigns?
- Is my discomfort spiritual guidance or just fear?

Integrity Framework:
- Assess if you can influence positive change in the role
- Consider alternative paths to financial relief
- Trust that declining may open doors to better opportunities

Possible Approaches: Sometimes the answer is to decline and trust that Allah has something better. Sometimes it's about creating change from within. The key is honest assessment of your ability to maintain your values.

## SCENARIO 2: THE SOCIAL PRESSURE

The Situation: Your child desperately wants to attend a birthday party where you know the environment won't align with your family's Islamic values—mixed gatherings with inappropriate activities, but all their friends will be there.

Heart-Check Questions:

- How can I honor my child's social needs while maintaining our boundaries?
- What creative alternatives could provide similar social connection?
- How do I explain our values without making my child feel restricted?

Integrity Framework:

- **Attend for a limited time that allows social connection while avoiding problematic activities**
- Offer to help plan alternative activities
- Create your own gatherings that align with your values

Possible Approaches: <u>Host</u>ing your own gathering with Islamic entertainment, arriving early and leaving before activities conflict with your values, or arranging alternative playdates with like-minded families.

## SCENARIO 3: THE BUSINESS PARTNERSHIP

The Situation: You've been making du'a to start your own business. A successful entrepreneur approaches you with a lucrative partnership opportunity in a field you're passionate about. However, during your conversations, they make subtle but persistent comments that reveal anti-Muslim bias—dismissing Islamic business practices, making "jokes" about your faith, or suggesting you'll need to "tone down the religious stuff" to succeed in their industry.

Heart-Check Questions:

- Can I maintain my Islamic identity and practices in this partnership?
- Will this person respect my values when difficult decisions arise?
- How would working closely with someone who disrespects my faith affect my spiritual wellbeing?

Integrity Framework:

- Address the bias directly and gauge their willingness to change
- Assess whether this partnership would require compromising your Islamic practices
- Consider finding partners who respect and share your values

Possible Approaches: Having an honest conversation about respect and boundaries, seeking business partnerships within the Muslim community, or pursuing the business opportunity independently rather than compromising your dignity and faith for financial gain.

## SCENARIO 4: THE INVESTMENT OPPORTUNITY

The Situation: You've been saving money and praying for wise investment opportunities. Your financial advisor recommends a mutual fund with excellent returns, but upon researching it, you find that it includes companies involved in tobacco, gambling, and arms manufacturing—industries that conflict with your values.

Heart-Check Questions:

- Can I truly benefit from something that causes harm to others?
- What message am I sending about my values through my financial choices?
- Am I prioritizing profit over principles?

Integrity Framework:

- Research ethical investment alternatives that match your values
- Accept potentially different returns for alignment with your principles
- Find a financial advisor who specializes in socially responsible investing

Possible Approaches: Values-based investments often perform well, and you gain peace of mind knowing your money supports companies whose missions align with your beliefs.

# REAL STORY OF HOLDING ON TO INTEGRITY IN LEAN SEASONS

After over twenty years as a compliance and ethics professional, I've learned that integrity isn't just about following rules—it's about navigating the gray areas where values meet reality. Throughout a career filled with writing codes of conduct and counselling organizations through ethical dilemmas, I've seen how even well-intentioned people can lose their way when pressure mounts. I've guided countless professionals through the difficult questions: What do you do when the "right" choice threatens your livelihood? How do you maintain your values when everyone around you is cutting corners?

This work has taught me that ethical decision-making requires more than policies—it requires a framework for thinking through complex situations. But the most powerful lesson came from my own life.

There have been times in my career as a consultant when money was tight—the nature of the business has its natural ebb and flow. During some of those lean seasons, clients or people that I had worked with in the past offered full-time employment that I turned down. Not because the jobs were haram (forbidden) but because they didn't align with the life I envisioned for myself.

I remember someone once asked me, "I don't understand how you can turn down work when you don't have money."

And my response was simple: "That's because you think I need more money than I think I do."

The opportunities I declined weren't unethical, but they would have compromised my ability to live my religion the way I wanted to. I wanted the freedom to attend Jumu'ah on Fridays. I wanted to stay up late for Tarawih prayers during Ramadan without having to punch a clock the next morning. I dreamed of spending Ramadan in Mecca. I didn't want to choose between earning a living and practicing my deen (religion).

Now, I'm not suggesting that everyone should quit their job to pursue these things. I had paid my dues as an employee. I was in a different stage of life. I had been praying for direction, and I truly believed that Allah had answered me. So, I quit my job, and I committed to not looking back during the lean times.

And in the end, Allah made a way for me. I've now been self-employed for over 15 years. That's barakah—divine blessing. When you prioritize purpose over money, when you act on the guidance you receive and trust Allah fully, He provides in ways you could never orchestrate on your own.

During these 15 years, I had the freedom to care for my mother in her final days and to support other family members in ways I couldn't have if I had been bound to a traditional job. I had the honor of living and working in Morocco for two years, experiencing daily life in a Muslim country. I spent part of Ramadan in Mecca, as I had dreamed of. And I had the time and space to write this book—and the one before it—both rooted in sharing the beauty of Islam.

And while I'm not doing exactly what I thought I'd be doing when I quit that job, I'm doing what I now believe Allah guided me to do.

None of this came from chasing money. It came from choosing alignment and trusting that when you walk in trust with Allah's plan, beautiful things unfold.

My journey taught me the importance of regularly examining our desires and goals through an Islamic lens. Before pursuing any major goal—whether it's a career change, business venture, or life decision—we need to ensure it aligns with our faith and values.

## Is My Desire Halal and Ethical? A Spiritual Check-In

When you're unsure whether a goal or method aligns with your faith, work through these seven tests. Each one helps you examine your intentions and approach from a different Islamic perspective:

## 1. The Permissibility Test

- Is what I want allowed in Islam?
- Is it free from haram actions or elements?
- Have I consulted knowledgeable sources about Islamic perspectives?

> *"O ye people! Eat of what is on earth, Lawful and good..."*
> (Qur'an 2:168)

## 2. The Method Test

- Am I harming anyone to achieve this goal?
- Am I being completely honest in my approach?
- Would I be comfortable if others knew my methods?

> *"Leave that which makes you doubt for that which does not make you doubt. Truth brings peace, and lies bring doubt."*
> (*Jami' at-Tirmidhi*, Book of Righteousness and Maintaining Good Relations, Hadith 2518)

## 3. The Purpose Test

- Will this draw me closer to Allah or distract me from Him?
- Does it serve a purpose beyond my own benefit?
- How will this affect my ability to worship and serve?

> *"And they have been commanded no more than this: To worship Allah, offering Him sincere devotion..."*
> (Qur'an 98:5)

## 4. The Surrender Test

- Would I be content if Allah gave me something different?
- Can I accept "no" or "not yet" with grace?
- Am I attached to the specific form this must take?

*"And if any one puts his trust in Allah, sufficient is (Allah) for him. For Allah will surely accomplish his purpose."*
(Qur'an 65:3)

## 5. The Istikhara Factor

- Have I sought Allah's guidance through the prayer of Istikhara?
- Am I willing to accept whatever guidance I receive?
- Have I made this decision after consulting Allah?

*"When one of you is concerned about a matter, let him pray two rak'ahs of voluntary prayer, then say: 'O Allah, I seek Your guidance through Your knowledge, and I seek ability through Your power, and I ask You of Your great bounty. You have power; I have none. And You know; I know not. You are the Knower of hidden things. O Allah, if in Your knowledge this matter is good for my religion, my livelihood and my affairs, immediate and in the future, then ordain it for me, make it easy for me, and bless it for me. And if in Your knowledge it is bad for my religion, my livelihood and my affairs, immediate and in the future, then turn it away from me, and turn me away from it. And ordain for me the good wherever it may be, and make me pleased with it.'"*
(*Sahih al-Bukhari*, Book of Tahajjud, Hadith 1162).

## 6. The Community Test

- What would righteous people in my community advise?
- Would I be comfortable discussing this with my imam?
- Am I setting a good example for other Muslims?

*"And hold fast, all together, by the rope which Allah (stretches out for you), and be not divided among yourselves."*
(Qur'an 3:103)

7. The Akhirah (the next life) Test

- Will I be proud of this choice when I meet Allah?
- How will I answer for this decision in the grave?
- Am I prioritizing temporary gains over eternal benefits?
- Does this help me become who Allah wants me to be?

*"But perhaps you hate a thing and it is good for you;*
*and perhaps you love a thing and it is bad for you.*
*And Allah knows, while you know not."*
(Qur'an 2:216)

## WHEN SUCCESS TESTS YOUR INTEGRITY

Sometimes the test isn't whether you'll get what you want, but whether you'll stay aligned when you're offered it. The real challenge may come when you're finally given what you asked for.

The Success Traps:

- **Rapid Growth:** Temptation to cut corners or forget your values
- **Recognition:** Pride creeping in, forgetting Allah's role
- **Financial Abundance:** You may find yourself so caught up enjoying the luxury lifestyle that you have less time for remembrance and prayer. The comfort can become a distraction from spiritual growth.

*"Know ye (all), that the life of this world is but play and*
*amusement, pomp and mutual boasting and multiplying,*
*(in rivalry) among yourselves, riches and children. Here is a*
*similitude: How rain and the growth which it brings forth,*
*delight (the hearts of) the tillers; soon it withers; thou wilt*
*see it grow yellow; then it becomes dry and crumbles away.*
*But in the Hereafter is a Penalty severe (for the devotees of*
*wrong). And Forgiveness from Allah and (His) Good*

*Pleasure (for the devotees of Allah). And what is the life of this world, but goods and chattels of deception?"*
(Qur'an 57:20)

You may see YOLO written or hear "You only live once," sometimes used as justification for haram activity. The live once part is accurate— but the one life that truly matters is the eternal life in the Hereafter. "So, when you see YOLO, don't think of this world, think of the next one. The Qur'an reminds us: *"And what is the worldly life except the enjoyment of delusion."* (Qur'an 57:20 Dr. Mustafa Khattab, The Clear Quran translation)

Questions for Self-Reflection:

- Am I compromising my *deen* (religion) for the sake of *dunya* (this world)?
- How would I explain this decision to Allah?
- Am I leading with my values or being led by my desires?

## REAL STORY OF A HUMBLING REMINDER AT THE MASJID

As I mentioned in the opening pages, this book is as much for me as it is for you. We are, by nature, forgetful beings who need constant reminders to keep our hearts aligned with divine truth.

I experienced this firsthand after buying a new car. When I purchased the car, I was thinking comfort, reliability, value, and beauty too. I wasn't thinking status. After I got the blessing, I found myself walking toward it with a sense of pride, thinking deep down, "People are noticing that I'm driving a nice car." Ego and pride were creeping in—exactly the kind of spiritual arrogance this book warns against.

But Allah blessed me with a swift reminder. The car was less than two months old when I parked in the underground garage at the masjid, near a concrete column. I walked past that column without really noticing it. I said it was because I was tired, but it was probably because I was too busy thinking about what people thought of me driving this car.

When I backed out of the parking space—*bam*—I dented my new car right against that column.

When I told a friend what happened, I said, "I think I was being too proud." She laughed and said, "Yup, and you got your reminder at the masjid, of all places." We both laughed. The arrogance was dented out of me. All I could say was "*Alhamdulillah*" (all praise is to Allah).

I drove around with that dent for three months before fixing it—not because I couldn't afford the repair, but because I needed the daily reminder. Every time I saw it, I remembered to stay humble about my blessings and grateful to the One who provides them. The dented car became a powerful symbol: when we lose sight of the Source of our blessings, we inevitably damage what we've been given. This is why maintaining integrity isn't just about the journey—it's about how we carry ourselves once we arrive.

## The Heart of Integrity

True abundance doesn't come from controlling life—it comes from trusting the One who controls it all. You don't need to chase what's meant for you. You don't need to fear delay. You just need to walk in alignment, with faith as your guide and integrity as your foundation.

## Spiritual Takeaway

You gain little if you lose your values while pursuing success. When you keep Allah at the center of your goals, your pursuit becomes worship. True manifestation doesn't mean getting what you want—it means becoming who Allah wants you to be while receiving what He knows is best for you. Living this way creates spiritual alignment.

## Journey Prompts

1. Where might your pursuit of a goal be pulling you away from your Islamic principles?

2. If success in your current path required a moral compromise, what would you choose?
3. Write about a time when choosing integrity cost you something valuable. How did Allah compensate you later?
4. This week, audit one area of your life for complete ethical alignment. Make necessary adjustments even if they're uncomfortable.

## AS WE CONTINUE THE JOURNEY

You've established integrity as the container for your manifestation practice, learning to keep Allah at the center even when it requires difficult choices. This ethical foundation is crucial, but you might be discovering that even with pure intentions and ethical alignment, something still feels stuck.

If you're like many sincere seekers, you understand the principles intellectually and try to live them authentically, yet you notice resistance—fear, doubt, or self-sabotage that seems to interfere with your spiritual progress.

This resistance isn't a sign of failure; it's an invitation to deeper healing. Often, the most significant barriers to receiving Allah's blessings aren't external circumstances—they're the internal blocks we've carried for years, sometimes without even realizing it. In our next chapter, we'll identify and clear these hidden obstacles that can create resistance between your heart and Allah's infinite mercy.

## DU'A

*"Ya Allah, protect my integrity. Let every step I take be rooted in obedience to You and guided by Your light. Help me pursue my goals in ways that bring me closer to You, not further away. May my success serve as a means of deepening my faith and enhancing my service to others."*

"Allah does not change
a people's lot unless
they change what is in their
hearts."
(Qur'an 13:11)

# CHAPTER ELEVEN
## CLEARING INTERNAL BLOCKS

You've learned to manifest with integrity, keeping Allah at the center of your goals and aspirations. But sometimes, even with pure intentions and sincere *du'a* (supplication), you might notice resistance that seems to interfere with your spiritual progress. Together we'll examine how to identify and clear the internal blocks that can create barriers between your heart and Allah's blessings.

Manifestation in the Islamic framework isn't only about asking; it's about becoming a vessel that's able and ready to receive. Often, the things you yearn for aren't being withheld but are waiting on the other side of something unaddressed: an old wound, an unhealed heartbreak, a hardened heart, or a whisper of disbelief.

## THE HEART AS THE SPIRITUAL CENTER

In Islam, the state of the heart (*qalb*) is central to everything. The Prophet (PBUH) said:

> *"Truly in the body, there is a morsel of flesh which, if it is sound, the whole body is sound; and if it is corrupt, the whole body is corrupt. Truly, it is the heart."*
> (*Sahih al-Bukhari*, Book of Belief, Hadith 52,
> Also in: *Sahih Muslim*, Book of Governance, Hadith 1599)

Your heart isn't just the emotional seat of your being—it's also the spiritual filter through which your du'a passes. When your heart is heavy with shame, grief, resentment, or self-doubt, it may become harder to feel a connection with Allah, to trust His response, or even to believe you're worthy of being heard.

The Qur'an speaks directly to this:

> *"Those who believe, and whose hearts find satisfaction in the remembrance of Allah: for without doubt in the remembrance of Allah do hearts find satisfaction."*
> (Qur'an 13:28)

But what happens when your heart feels anything but assured? When does past pain cloud your ability to trust? When negative self-talk drowns out the quiet voice of hope?

## UNDERSTANDING INTERNAL BLOCKS

Internal blocks are the unconscious barriers that prevent you from fully engaging with your du'a practice, trusting Allah's response, or believing you deserve His mercy. They often manifest in different ways:

**Spiritual Blocks**
- Doubt in Allah's mercy: "My sins are too great for forgiveness"
- Feeling unworthy: "Allah won't answer my prayers"
- Past unanswered du'as: "Prayer doesn't work for me"
- Spiritual perfectionism: "I'm not religious enough to ask for anything"
- Fear of testing: "If I get what I want, Allah might test me with loss"

**Emotional Blocks**
- Chronic self-doubt: "I don't deserve good things"
- Fear of disappointment: "It's safer not to hope"
- Unprocessed grief: From loss, betrayal, or broken dreams
- Comparison and envy: "Everyone else gets blessed but me"
- Shame from past mistakes: "I've made too many wrong choices"

**Mental Blocks**
- Scarcity mindset: "There's not enough to go around"

- All-or-nothing thinking: "If it's not exactly as I imagined, it's not from Allah"
- Catastrophic thinking: "If I get my hopes up, something terrible will happen"
- Imposter syndrome: "I'm fooling myself if I think I can achieve this"
- Control addiction: "I need to know exactly how and when things will happen"

Cultural and Family Blocks

- Cultural expectations: "Good Muslims don't want worldly things"
- Family trauma: Patterns of fear, limitation, or dysfunction passed down through generations
- Gender limitations: "Women/men shouldn't aspire to certain things"
- Socioeconomic conditioning: "People like us don't get those opportunities"
- Religious guilt: "Wanting this makes me a bad Muslim"

---

### ! IMPORTANT DISCLAIMER

This chapter discusses how emotional pain can affect spiritual practice. While I share personal insights and reference research, this is not professional mental health advice. If you're struggling with trauma, please seek help from qualified mental health professionals, particularly those who understand your faith perspective.

---

## TRAUMA, DOUBT, AND UNHEALED PAIN AS BARRIERS TO DU'A

This next part might seem a bit academic, but bear with me, because it addresses an important reality that many of us face—how emotional pain can create barriers in our spiritual lives.

You don't need to be a therapist to recognize that deep emotional pain can leave lasting impressions—not just on the body, but on the soul. I don't write this as a clinician but as someone who has lived through grief and disorientation—and who has witnessed how personal pain can impact a person's ability to hope, trust, or even pray.

Some people find that difficult life experiences influence how they relate to themselves, others, and even Allah. These experiences might make trust feel unsafe, dim hope, and sometimes trigger a quiet crisis of faith.

Modern trauma research offers insights into this. In The Body Keeps the Score, Dr. Bessel van der Kolk explains that trauma can alter our perception of safety, connection, and meaning in the world. If unhealed, these patterns might carry over into how we relate to Allah, especially when our pain is connected to what felt like unanswered prayers.

While modern research helps us understand how trauma affects the mind and body, our Islamic tradition teaches us that Allah is Al-Jabbar (The One who mends what is broken). The path to healing can beautifully integrate both psychological understanding and spiritual reliance, allowing us to seek professional help while trusting in Allah's ultimate power to restore what has been damaged.

## WHEN DIFFICULT EXPERIENCES BECOME SPIRITUAL BARRIERS

Sometimes, painful experiences can create an invisible wall between you and your ability to believe that good is possible. You might begin to internalize fear, doubt, or unworthiness that influences how you ask Allah for what you want—or whether you ask at all.

Here are some ways difficult experiences can affect our spiritual practice:

- People who experienced abandonment might find it challenging to trust fully, even in Allah, with du'as carrying an undertone of "Please don't leave me too."

- Those who grew up with conditional affection may unconsciously feel they must "earn" Allah's mercy through perfect behavior.
- After experiencing betrayal, some may push blessings away, fearing that nothing good ever lasts.
- If basic needs went unmet in childhood, they might struggle to believe they're worthy of having them met now.
- Negative experiences with religious figures or communities can make people hesitant to ask Allah for anything beyond basic survival.

This can also contribute to painful spiritual questioning when prayers seem unanswered—a parent losing a child despite prayer, a marriage ending despite desperate du'as, or anxiety increasing rather than decreasing despite seeking Allah's help.

If you are in a place of questioning Allah's mercy or experiencing emotional pain, I make this du'a for you: "May Allah ease your pain, lighten your burdens, and make what is difficult easy." The fact that you are reading this means you still believe in the power of du'a, even if just a little. *Alhamdulillah* (all praise is to Allah). That spark is enough.

These aren't signs of weak faith—they're often echoes of a wounded heart seeking understanding.

## WHAT SCHOLARS AND EXPERTS SAY

Dr. Rania Awaad, a Stanford psychiatrist and Islamic scholar, notes that trauma can disrupt a person's relationship with Allah, causing shame, spiritual numbness, or detachment. Healing requires addressing both psychological and spiritual dimensions.

Abu Zayd al-Balkhi, a 9th-century Muslim scholar, wrote extensively on emotional and spiritual health, recognizing sadness, anxiety, and fear as real conditions requiring comprehensive care.

Dr. Bessel van der Kolk explains that trauma reshapes how we think, feel, and connect—and that healing is possible when we gently reintegrate the body and brain with safety, ritual, and meaning.

Healing Is Part of Faith. Islam recognizes emotional and psychological pain. The Prophet Muhammad (PBUH) wept, grieved, and sought solitude. He taught us that the heart matters and that true strength comes not from suppressing pain but from seeking Allah through it.

## PROFESSIONAL HELP AND ISLAMIC HEALING

Some Muslims believe that mental health issues can be resolved solely through prayer and spiritual practice. While du'a is indeed powerful and healing, sometimes the mental health condition itself becomes the barrier that makes it difficult to pray, trust, or connect spiritually.

Depression can make it hard to feel hope. Anxiety can make it difficult to trust Allah's plan. Trauma can create barriers to believing you're worthy of Allah's mercy. In these cases, seeking professional help isn't a sign of weak faith—it's using the means Allah has provided for healing.

Just as you would seek medical treatment for a broken bone while also making du'a for healing, mental health deserves the same integrated approach. Allah has given us both du'a and doctors, both prayer and professional expertise. Using all available tools shows wisdom, not weakness.

When to seek professional help:
- If emotional pain significantly interferes with daily life
- If you have thoughts of self-harm
- If trauma memories are overwhelming
- If you're unable to function normally

Remember to seek qualified mental health professionals who understand and respect your faith perspective.

## THE WAY FORWARD

Healing from difficult experiences doesn't mean erasing the past; it means learning how to carry it differently. Understanding how these experiences affect our spiritual life is only the first step.

## SPIRITUAL TAKEAWAY

Allah is *Al-Fattah*—the Opener of all doors. But sometimes, the door that must open first is within your own heart. Internal blocks—whether emotional pain, doubt, or shame—can cloud your trust in Allah's love and your worthiness to receive His blessings. Healing isn't separate from your manifestation journey; it is a part of the journey.

## JOURNEY PROMPTS

1. What negative belief about yourself or Allah's mercy keeps surfacing when you make du'a?
2. How might childhood experiences or past disappointments be affecting your ability to receive?
3. Write a compassionate letter to the part of you that feels unworthy of Allah's blessings. Remind yourself of His infinite mercy.
4. This week, when self-doubt arises, counter it with this: "Allah's mercy is greater than my mistakes. His love is stronger than my fears."

## AS WE CONTINUE THE JOURNEY

You've done great work identifying and recognizing that you must clear the internal blocks that can create barriers to receiving Allah's blessings. This healing journey deserves recognition—confronting old wounds and limiting beliefs requires courage and spiritual maturity.

But here's the reality that many people discover: insights without consistent practice fade like morning mist.

The most beautiful spiritual breakthrough means nothing if it doesn't translate into how you live each day. Transformation isn't a moment—it's a thousand small moments of choosing alignment over convenience, remembrance over distraction, trust over fear.

In our next chapter, we'll create a sustainable daily practice that makes Islamic manifestation not just an occasional spiritual experience but a natural way of being. These aren't overwhelming routines you'll abandon in two weeks—they're simple, powerful practices that can become as natural as breathing.

## DU'A

*"Ya Allah, remove the doubts and wounds that distance me from Your mercy. Heal my heart so I can receive from You fully. Help me release what no longer serves my growth and fill the empty spaces with trust in Your love for me. Make me a clear vessel, ready to receive the blessings You have written for me.*

"And do thou (O reader!) Bring thy Lord to remembrance in thy (very) soul, with humility and in reverence, without loudness in words, in the mornings and evenings; and be not thou of those who are unheedful."
(Qur'an 7:205)

# CHAPTER TWELVE
## A DAILY PRACTICE—LIVING YOUR DU'A IN SACRED RHYTHM

You've journeyed through the complete seven-step framework. You've learned to visualize with intention (*niyyah*), ask with sincerity, believe (*yaqeen*), act with purpose, trust in Allah (*tawakkul*), surrender with contentment (*rida*), and receive with gratitude (*shukr*). You've explored how to maintain integrity and clear internal blocks. Now comes a very challenging part: living it.

Islam teaches us that consistency, not intensity, is the path to Allah's pleasure. The Prophet (PBUH) said:

> *"The most beloved deeds to Allah are those*
> *that are consistent, even if small."*
> (*Sahih al-Bukhari*, Book of Riqaq, Hadith 6464,
> Also in: Sahih Muslim, Book of Salat al-Musafirin, Hadith
> 782)

This chapter brings it all together—your du'a, your *niyyah* (intention), your *tawakkul* (trust in Allah), your *shukr* (gratitude), and your alignment. It's about creating a rhythm that supports your values, your vision, and your spiritual growth. These aren't just habits—they're sacred practices that keep your heart connected to Allah while your hands work toward your goals.

## YOUR DAILY DU'A PRACTICE

Before diving into complex routines, let's establish some foundational elements that connect your long-term vision with daily spiritual discipline. This approach isn't about perfection—it's about consistency and sincerity.

## STEP 1: CHOOSE YOUR VISION HORIZON

Decide on a timeframe that feels most meaningful for your journey—1, 2, or 3 years. This becomes the timeframe for your vision-centered du'as. Which timeframe should you choose? That depends on your goals and where you are in life.

- 1 year - Immediate alignment: Perfect if you're entering a new season—career shift, health goal, renewed spiritual focus—and want to see progress more quickly.
- 2 years - Deep development: Balanced timeframe for meaningful change in relationships, education, business growth, or long-term healing.
- 3 years - Transformation and legacy: Best for major life shifts like homeownership, marriage, spiritual mastery, or legacy-building. This timeframe also works well if you're looking to work on different dimensions of yourself simultaneously, like family, career, and growing a business. It invites spacious trust in Allah's perfect timing.

Choose the timeframe that resonates with your heart, and let your vision reflect that sacred horizon.

## STEP 2: WRITE YOUR TOP 10 DU'AS

You have already been focusing on *du'as* (supplication)throughout this journey. Now it is time to select your top ones. Before starting daily practices, write your top 10 du'as for your chosen timeframe. These are the heartfelt goals and dreams you bring to Allah—make them specific, meaningful, and spiritually aligned. If you need help coming up with your ten, try free writing.

Free Writing Technique: This creates space for *tafakkur* (contemplation), helping you hear the quiet voice of your *fitrah* (natural disposition). Write whatever is on your heart—questions, frustrations, hopes, or prayers. If you don't know what to write, begin with: "Ya Allah, I feel..." Let your words lead you to clarity and deeper self-awareness.

Once you've written your Top 10 du'as, you're ready for daily practice. Remember, your priorities may shift over time, and that's perfectly natural. You evolve. Your du'as evolve with you.

## MORNING ROUTINE: BEGIN WITH BISMILLAH

### BASIC MORNING RITUAL (10 - 20 MINUTES):

1. Wake with gratitude: "Alhamdulillah al-ladhi ahyana ba'da ma amatana wa ilayhi al-nushur." (All praise is to Allah who gave us life after having taken it from us, and unto Him is the resurrection.)

2. Begin your morning routine with Bismillah al-Rahman al-Raheem: "In the name of Allah, the Most Merciful, the Most Compassionate."

3. Set conscious intentions: Take 5-10 minutes to center yourself through stillness or silent meditation. Meditation softens the heart and quiets the noise. In stillness, you remember that Allah is near. Note: Use a timer.

4. Make du'a: Ask Allah to guide your words, steps, and decisions for the day.

5. Write in your journal:
   o What is my intention today?
   o What kind of person do I want to be today (with myself, with others, with Allah)?
   o What is one small act I can do today that aligns with my larger vision?

*Example: "Today, I intend to approach my work with excellence and gratitude, trusting that Allah will bless my efforts with barakah."*

**Expanding Your Practice:** As you grow consistent with the basics, layer in:

- Two rak'ah of voluntary prayer
- Reading or listening to the Qur'an
- Visualizing your answered du'a and speaking it aloud with conviction
- Daily affirmation: "O Allah, I intend to walk in integrity, serve where I'm needed, and stay grounded in Your remembrance. Guide me, protect me, and open doors that are good for me." You can use this or create your own.

**Morning Tips:** If you have a busy or full house that makes morning rituals difficult, try waking up a few minutes earlier than the rest of the house. Or attach this practice to your Fajr prayer routine when you're already in a spiritual mindset.

## MIDDAY RESET: DHUHR AS YOUR SPIRITUAL CHECKPOINT (5 - 10 MINUTES)

Use the rhythm of salah to re-center your soul. Let Dhuhr (midday prayer) become a checkpoint for alignment:

1. **Ask:** Are my actions aligned with my values and vision?
2. **Recite:** A short du'a or engage in dhikr such as *SubhanAllah* (glory be to Allah), *Alhamdulillah* (all praise is due to Allah), *Allah hu* (He is Allah) *Akbar* (Allah is the Greatest). If you don't already have a practice of dhikr, start small with repeating each phrase 33 times. Work your way up to 99, plus 1. You can use prayer beads, count on your fingers, or use a manual or smart finger counter.
3. **Revisit:** Your morning intention to course-correct with compassion.

This midday pause keeps you connected to your spiritual center throughout busy days.

> *"Guard strictly your (habit of) prayers, especially the Middle Prayer; and stand before Allah in a devout (frame of mind)."*
> (Qur'an 2:238)

Midday Tips: This is an important check-in time. For most of us, midday is when we have the most contact with the outside world—subject to influences, distractions, and work demands. The Qur'an says to protect your middle prayer, and many believe that this is one of reason- It serves as a spiritual reset during the most demanding hours. Attach this practice to a routine you already have: Dhuhr prayer or lunch break.

## EVENING REFLECTION: RETURN TO GRATITUDE

### BASIC EVENING RITUAL (5 - 10 MINUTES):

1. Make du'a: Ask Allah to accept what was good, forgive what fell short, and purify your heart.
2. Write in your journal:
   o What am I grateful for today?
   o Where did I see Allah's presence in my day?
   o What could I do differently tomorrow with more awareness?

*Example: "I noticed how calm I felt when I paused to make dhikr (remembrance of Allah) in traffic. That moment reminded me that peace is always available when I remember Allah."*

Expanding Your Evening Practice: As you become consistent, layer in:

- Meditate: Engage in timed meditation - choose one of these rhythmic remembrances:
  o *"SubhanAllah"* (glory be to Allah) with each inhale, *"Alhamdulillah"* (all praise is due to Allah) with each exhale
  o *"Allah Hu"* (He is Allah) - breathing "Allah" on the inhale and "Hu" on the exhale, affirming His presence and transcendence
- Journal: moments of peace, purpose, or spiritual clarity
- Reflect: How did I walk in alignment with my du'a today?

- Make du'a: Offer heartfelt supplications for consistency, clarity, and surrender to divine timing

Evening Tips: Find that quiet time before you sleep or ask family for 10 minutes of privacy. This works well after you put the kids to sleep, when the house naturally becomes more peaceful and reflective.

## WEEKLY & MONTHLY ALIGNMENT

### WEEKLY RITUAL:

- Choose 1-2 du'as from your Top 10 to focus on each week. It's okay to repeat the same ones for several weeks or return to them later. Move on when it feels right.
- Reflect: Am I taking inspired steps? Am I surrendering what I cannot control?
- Use Jumu'ah as a time for deeper spiritual alignment and community connection. While women aren't required to attend Jumu'ah, it offers a powerful weekly reset for those who can participate. This is especially beneficial if you're living and working around non-Muslims throughout the week, as it provides an opportunity to connect with the Muslim community and receive spiritual nourishment through the khutbah.

### MONTHLY CHECK-INS:

- Review your Top 10 Du'as and refine them as your clarity and circumstances evolve
- Reflect on answered prayers and spiritual shifts
- Celebrate progress and acknowledge areas for growth

## WHEN LIFE DISRUPTS YOUR ROUTINE

Consistency doesn't mean perfection. When you miss a day or feel spiritually distant:

- Return without guilt: Allah's mercy is always there

- Start small: Even one du'a or moment of gratitude counts
- Adjust, don't abandon: Modify your practice to fit your current season
- Remember your why: Reconnect with your original intention for this journey

The Prophet (PBUH) reminded us:

---

*"Take up good deeds only as much as you are able, for the best of deeds is that which is done consistently even if it is small."*
(*Sunan Ibn Majah*, Book of Book of Zuhd, Hadith 4240)

---

## ADVANCED INTEGRATION PRACTICES

### ADDITIONAL SPIRITUAL PRACTICES

- Gratitude Circles: Gather trusted friends to share goals, make du'a for each other, and celebrate wins together
- Service Integration: Use your skills and blessings to serve others as a form of gratitude
- Seasonal Reflection: Use Islamic calendar events such as *Ramadan* (month of fasting), or Hajj season for deeper spiritual alignment

## SPIRITUAL TAKEAWAY

Allah loves consistency in small deeds. Your daily habits aren't just tasks—they're spiritual scaffolding that prepares your heart to receive divine gifts. Your daily rhythms become your quiet covenant with Allah: to show up, remember, ask, and trust.

---

## JOURNEY PROMPTS

1. What time of day feels most sacred to you for spiritual practice? What makes it special?

2. What's one practice from this chapter that resonates deeply with your lifestyle and personality?
3. Design your ideal daily spiritual routine, including morning, midday, and evening practices. Keep it simple and sustainable.
4. This week, implement just the morning portion of your routine. Master this before adding more.

## AS WE CONTINUE THE JOURNEY

Now that you have your top 10 du'as and have established daily practices that create a sacred rhythm in your life, it's time to give your prayers a visual dimension. In the next chapter, we'll explore how to create a vision board with taqwa—transforming your heartfelt du'as into a tangible reminder that keeps your intentions focused and your heart connected to Allah's guidance.

## DU'A

*"O Allah, I intend to walk in integrity, serve where I'm needed, and stay grounded in Your remembrance. Guide me, protect me, and open doors that are good for me. Let my actions today bring me closer to the vision You have written for me, and help me surrender what is not mine to control. Ameen."*

"And We shall try you until We test those
among you who strive their utmost and persevere in patience; and We shall try your reported (mettle)."
(Qur'an 47:31)

# CHAPTER THIRTEEN
## VISION BOARD WITH TAQWA

You've learned to make *du'a* (supplication) with consistency and sincerity. Now, let's explore how you can give your supplications a visual dimension that deepens your connection to your intentions. Creating a vision board is a remarkable way to bring your dreams into focus, but when you approach it with *taqwa* (God-consciousness), it becomes something much more sacred than typical manifestation tools.

While digital vision boards can be convenient, there's something uniquely empowering about creating a physical board with your own hands. The act of cutting, pasting, writing, and arranging images and words allows you to connect with your intentions on a deeper level. When done with the right *niyyah* (intention), it can become a form of meditation and worship.

A Vision Board with Taqwa isn't just a place to put wishes. It's a tactile representation of what your du'a looks like when translated into visual form. The vision board allows you to:

- Reflect on your true desires
- Organize your spiritual priorities
- Pray with greater clarity and focus

## EMBRACE THE TACTILE PROCESS

There's something about working with your hands that engages more than just your mind. When you create a vision board physically, you're involving multiple senses in the process of clarifying your intentions:

Engage your senses: The texture of the paper, the scent of the glue, and the feel of the scissors in your hand—all of these sensory experiences can enhance your connection to the process and make it feel more real and grounded.

Slow down and be mindful: Creating a physical vision board requires you to take the time to slow down and be intentional about each step. This mindfulness can help you clarify your intentions and connect with Allah on a deeper level. You can't rush through cutting and pasting the way you might click and drag digital images.

Connect with your creativity: The act of creating something with your hands can be a form of worship, allowing you to express your gratitude and connect with Allah's creative power. As you arrange and rearrange elements, you're participating in the divine act of bringing order from chaos.

Seeing the Divine Connections: When I'm putting together a vision board, I'm always looking to see how the pieces work together—the different aspects of my life, the different dreams. I observe how the financial goals fuel the travel aspirations, how travel contributes to my health and spiritual growth, how my living space accommodates spiritual practices, and how my work serves both my material needs and my desire to help others. This holistic view reflects the Islamic understanding that all aspects of life should work in harmony to serve our ultimate purpose of worshipping and pleasing Allah.

Creating a vision board with taqwa means seeing your life as an integrated whole rather than separate compartments. Your career should support your spiritual growth, your relationships should bring you closer to Allah, your health should enable you to serve better, and your dreams should align with divine purpose. As you place each element on your board, ask yourself: "How does this piece connect to my other goals? How does this serve my *dunya* (this world) and *akhirah* (the next life)?"

## WHAT TO INCLUDE

The steps that we are about to take is where your vision board differs from secular manifestation tools. Gather magazines, newspapers, printed images, inspiring quotes, fabric scraps, dried flowers—anything that resonates with your vision. But as you create your board, focus on images and words that reflect taqwa and a life that is pleasing to Allah.

Words that reflect Islamic values:

- *Barakah* (blessing), *sakinah* (tranquility), ease
- *Sabr* (patience), *rida* (contentment), service to others
- Remembrance of Allah, gratitude, community

Images that evoke spiritual connection:

- Scenes that remind you of Allah's creation and beauty
- Images of family, community, and service
- Visual representations of the feelings you want to cultivate
- Places where you can worship and grow spiritually

Qur'anic verses or Hadith that inspire you:

- Verses about provision, guidance, and divine mercy
- Prophetic sayings about good character and righteous goals
- Reminders of your relationship with Allah

Reminders of your values and priorities as a Muslim:

- Images that represent halal success and ethical achievement
- Visual cues that remind you of your purpose as Allah's servant
- Elements that connect your worldly goals to your spiritual growth

Avoid focusing solely on material items or worldly achievements. Instead, focus on the qualities and experiences that will bring you closer to Allah and help you fulfill your purpose in this life.

## THE SPIRITUAL DIMENSION

Creating a Vision Board with Taqwa, when done with sincerity and mindfulness, becomes more than a planning tool—it becomes a tangible representation of your du'a, a constant reminder of your intentions, and a crucial aid for connecting with Allah.

Visualization, in and of itself, isn't unique to Islam. But it becomes a spiritual discipline when you pair it with sincere niyyah, heartfelt humility, and complete submission to Allah's will. Your goal isn't to control the outcome or manipulate reality but to clarify your prayer, center Allah in your desire, remember that He alone is Ar-Razzaq, and walk forward in trust, knowing that even if the outcome is different from what you imagined, Allah's plan is always better.

> *"And your Lord says, 'Call upon Me; I will respond to you.'"*
> (Qur'an 40:60)

So, visualize with intention and mindfulness. Then, ask Allah with sincerity. Then, trust in His wisdom and plan. And walk as though the One you're calling on already knows the way and will guide you toward what is best.

## CREATING YOUR SACRED CANVAS

Now that you understand the spiritual foundation of a Vision Board with Taqwa, it's time to bring your du'a into physical form. Your vision board can be as unique as your relationship with Allah—there's no single "right" way to create it, but there are practical considerations that will help you design something meaningful and sustainable.

### CHOOSE YOUR CANVAS SIZE

- **Poster Board (22" x 28")**: Perfect for a comprehensive life vision that covers multiple areas. This size gives you plenty of room to organize different life domains while maintaining visual clarity.
- **Cork Board (12" x 18")**: Ideal for a focused approach or smaller living spaces. This size works well when you want to concentrate on one or two specific areas of growth.

- Journal or Notebook Pages (8.5" x 11"): Create a portable vision board that travels with you. Perfect for those who prefer privacy or want to update their board frequently.
- Three-Panel Display Board (36" x 48" when open): A tri-fold board that creates a dedicated sacred space for your vision. This format allows you to organize your life into three main sections while creating a sense of enclosure and focus when you sit before it.
- Digital Frame Size (8" x 10"): A compact option that fits easily on a desk, nightstand, or prayer space without overwhelming the area.

## THE POWER OF PHYSICAL CREATION

As mentioned earlier, while digital vision boards are convenient, there's profound wisdom in using your hands whenever possible. The tactile process of cutting, arranging, and gluing engages your senses in a way that deepens your connection to your intentions. When you physically handle each element—feeling the texture of the paper, making deliberate choices about placement—you're creating muscle memory of your du'a.

If circumstances truly require a digital approach—perhaps you're frequently traveling, have limited storage space, or lack access to physical materials—consider using a digital photo frame that you can easily update. The key is that your vision board remains readily available for daily reflection, not buried in a computer file or phone gallery where it might be forgotten.

Your vision board can take two main approaches, both spiritually valid:

The Focused Board concentrates on one area of life where you're seeking Allah's guidance and *barakah* (blessing):

- Financial: *Halal* (permissible) wealth, debt freedom, generous giving, ethical business success
- Family: Marriage, children, strengthening family bonds, creating a loving Islamic home

- Career: Meaningful work, professional growth, using your talents to serve Allah
- Health: Physical wellness, mental peace, spiritual vitality, caring for Allah's *amanah* (trust)
- Travel: Hajj, Umrah, exploring Allah's creation, meaningful journeys
- Education: Islamic knowledge, professional development, teaching others

The Integrated Board reflects the Islamic principle that all aspects of life should work in harmony to serve Allah: This approach helps you see the connections between different areas—how your career can fund your Hajj, how your health enables your service to others, how your family relationships strengthen your faith, and how your financial goals can increase your ability to give charity.

When creating an integrated board, organize your elements so they flow naturally from one area to another, showing how each aspect of your life supports your overall purpose as Allah's servant.

## PREPARING YOUR SACRED SPACE

Before you begin cutting and pasting, create an environment conducive to mindful creation:

- Choose a quiet time when you won't be rushed
- Begin with a brief du'a asking Allah to guide your intentions
- Have your materials ready: magazines, printouts, scissors, glue, markers
- Keep your prayer beads or Qur'an nearby as reminders of your spiritual focus

Whether you choose a single focus or integrated approach, remember that this board represents your active du'a—a visual conversation with Allah about the life you're asking Him to help you create.

# VISION BOARD TEMPLATES

*Add images, du'as, Qur'an quotes, goals and dreams*

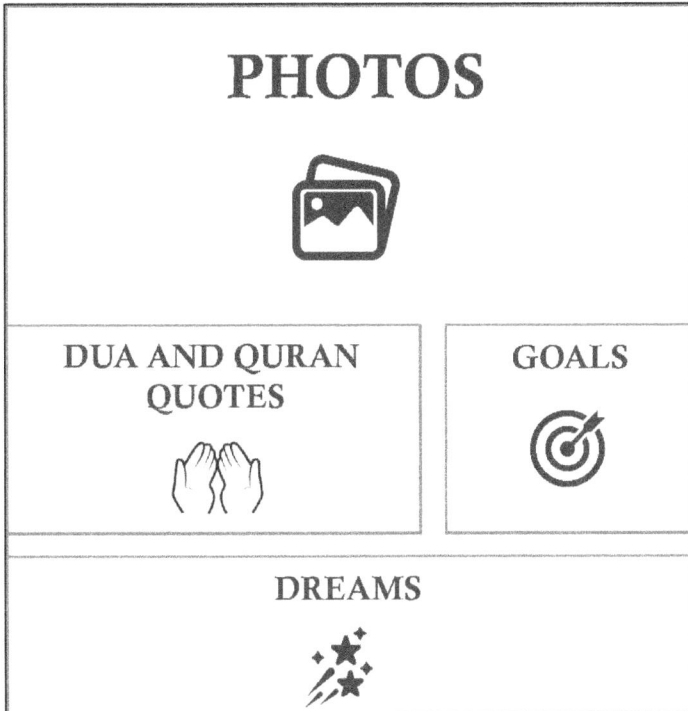

## PHOTOS

### DUA AND QURAN QUOTES

### GOALS

### DREAMS

| SPIRITUAL | CAREER |
|:---:|:---:|
|  |  |

| FAMILY | HEALTH |
|:---:|:---:|
|  |  |

| WEALTH | KNOWLEDGE |
|:---:|:---:|
|  | |

| RELATIONSHIP | TRAVEL |
|:---:|:---:|
|  |  |

*Add images, du'as, Qur'an quotes, goals and dreams*

## ADVANCED INTEGRATION PRACTICES

Revisit your vision board regularly—not as a wish list, but as a living reflection of your du'a, action, trust, and surrender. Align your goals with *akhlaq* (character), *ikhlas* (sincerity), and *tawakkul* (trust in Allah).

## Spiritual Takeaway

A vision board created with taqwa becomes a bridge between your heart's desires and your Creator's perfect plan. It's not about demanding specific outcomes but about clarifying your intentions so you can ask Allah with greater focus and surrender the results with greater trust.

## Journey Prompts

1. What area of your life feels most in need of clarity right now? Describe what you are asking Allah for in this area—and what surrendering the outcome would look like.

2. What words or Qur'anic verses most reflect the kind of life you're praying to live? Write them out and reflect on why they resonate with your goals.

3. Choose one image or word you'd include on your vision board. Now ask: How does this image serve both my dunya and akhirah?

4. What intentions do you need to renew before creating your board?

5. Reflect on how your board can be an act of worship—not wish-making.

## As We Continue the Journey

You've learned to live your du'a daily and give it visual form through mindful creation; you understand that your vision board isn't a magic charm—it's a tool for focused worship and spiritual alignment. You've established daily practices that create a sacred rhythm in your life, making Islamic manifestation a living part of your relationship with Allah.

This consistency is beautiful—but life rarely stays consistent. What happens when your carefully crafted routines get disrupted by a family crisis? How do you maintain spiritual alignment during a career transition, a health challenge, or a major move? When your elderly parent needs care, your job demands change, or unexpected financial stress arrives—do the principles you've learned only work in ideal circumstances?

As you look at your vision board—those images and words representing your deepest hopes—you might wonder: "Can this really happen for me during difficult times? How do I keep faith when life feels chaotic?"

The actual test of any spiritual practice isn't how well it serves you during peaceful times—it's how it sustains you through every season of life. The path ahead reveals how to adapt your manifestation framework to real-life situations, ensuring that whether you're navigating abundance or scarcity, celebration or grief, your connection to Allah and your ability to align with His will remain strong and flexible.

## DU'A

*"Ya Allah, guide my hands and heart as I create this visual reminder of my hopes and dreams. Let it serve as a tool that draws me closer to You and helps me ask for what is truly best for my deen, my dunya, and my akhirah."*

"O ye who believe! Celebrate the praises
of Allah, and do this often; And
glorify Him morning and evening."
(Qur'an 33:41-42)

# CHAPTER FOURTEEN
## MANIFESTATION THROUGH LIFE'S SEASONS

Your daily practices provide the foundation, but life unfolds in seasons—each with its unique rhythm, challenges, and spiritual lessons. Don't reserve the seven-step manifestation framework you've learned just for ideal circumstances. It supports you through all of life's transitions—whether you're navigating a career change, grieving a loss, welcoming new beginnings, or waiting for clarity.

Manifestation in Islam isn't about controlling outcomes; it's about remaining anchored in divine trust and purpose through every phase of life. The process stays the same—visualize, ask, believe, act, trust, surrender, receive—but how you apply it shifts depending on your circumstances.

## LIFE TRANSITIONS AS SPIRITUAL TRAINING GROUNDS

Allah, in His wisdom, allows us to go through seasons that stretch us—not to harm us, but to draw us closer to Him. Whether you are seeking a new job, healing from heartbreak, facing illness, or grieving a loss, each season is an opportunity to apply your tools of *du'a* (supplication), *tawakkul* (trust), and purposeful action in a new way.

# CAREER TRANSITIONS AND PROFESSIONAL GROWTH

## THE JOB SEARCH SEASON

When you find yourself unexpectedly unemployed or seeking new opportunities, it can feel overwhelming. But this season often becomes a time for spiritual growth and manifestation practice.

Your Seven-Step Framework:

1. Visualize with Niyyah: Spend time in *tafakkur* (Contemplation), reflecting on what type of work would bring you closer to Allah. Envision yourself in a role where you can uphold Islamic principles while making a meaningful contribution.

2. Ask with Du'a: "Ya Allah, guide me to work that is halal, fulfilling, and allows me to support my family while growing in my *deen* (religion). If this transition is redirection toward something better, help me see the wisdom in it."

3. Believe with Yaqeen: Despite anxiety, remember that Allah is *Ar-Razzaq* (The Provider) and that your provision is already written. Practice daily affirmations rooted in Qur'anic verses.

---

**Quick Reference: Islamic Terms**

Niyyah - Conscious, purposeful intention to act for the sake of Allah

Tafakkur - Deep contemplation or reflection on Allah's signs and guidance

Du'a - Supplication; direct, personal prayer to Allah

Deen - Religion or complete way of life as prescribed by Islam

Yaqeen - Unwavering certainty and conviction in Allah's promises and plan

Ar-Razzaq - One of Allah's beautiful names meaning "The Provider"

Amal - Righteous deeds or actions performed in accordance with Islamic teachings

Tawakkul - Complete trust and reliance on Allah while taking appropriate action

Rida - Contentment and acceptance of Allah's decree with grace and serenity

Sabr - Patience, perseverance, and steadfastness through trials and difficulties

Shukr - Gratitude expressed through heart, tongue, and actions

4. **Act with Amal:** Update your resume, network within the Muslim professional community, apply strategically to companies whose values align with yours, and use the time for skill development.

5. **Trust with Tawakkul:** When interviews don't immediately lead to offers, remember that Allah's timing is perfect. Continue efforts while releasing attachment to specific outcomes.

6. **Surrender with Rida:** Accept that this transition might take longer than expected, and use the time to strengthen your relationship with Allah and your family.

7. **Receive with Shukr:** When opportunities arise, recognize them as gifts from Allah and express gratitude through both words and actions.

# GRIEF AND LOSS

## NAVIGATING THE SEASON OF SORROW

When you've lost someone dear or experienced a significant loss, manifestation might feel impossible. Yet this season, while painful, can deepen your reliance on Allah and clarify what truly matters.

Your Seven-Step Framework:

1. **Visualize with Niyyah:** In early grief, simply visualize moments of peace and Allah's mercy surrounding you. Later, you might envision healing and how your experience could help others.

2. **Ask with Du'a:** "Ya Allah, grant me sabr (patience) through this trial. Help me find meaning in this pain and draw me closer to You. Make this a source of purification and spiritual growth."

3. **Believe with Yaqeen:** Trust that Allah's wisdom encompasses what you cannot understand. Believe that your loved one is in a better place and that this separation is temporary.

4. **Act with Amal:** Take gentle action—allow yourself to grieve while maintaining basic spiritual practices. Seek counselling if needed. Connect with supportive community members.

5. **Trust with Tawakkul:** Release the need to understand "why" immediately. Trust that Allah's plan includes both difficulty and ease, and that He will not burden you beyond your capacity.

6. **Surrender with Rida:** Accept the reality of loss while maintaining hope in Allah's mercy. Surrender your timeline for healing to Allah's perfect timing.

7. **Receive with Shukr:** As healing gradually comes, receive it with gratitude. Look for the spiritual gifts hidden within your trial—increased empathy, deeper faith, stronger community bonds.

## REAL STORY OF WHEN GRIEF OVERWHELMED EVERYTHING

My sister's death hit me harder than I expected. Maybe it was because I was exhausted from caring for her in her final days, or because she had battled cancer for two years—and those were two years of anticipatory grief slowly wearing me down.

Even though I tried to maintain my normal routines, everything felt different. Grief wasn't just an emotion; it was rewiring my entire body. My voice became hoarse—I didn't even know that grief could affect your vocal cords like that. I started grinding my teeth while I slept, causing mouth problems that added physical pain to the emotional weight I was carrying. I continued my workouts, but I had to adjust them significantly. My trainer would ask me each session, "Where's your energy today?" For months, I would answer honestly: "50%... 60%..." Some days it felt like even less.

I was applying what would later become the framework I've shared with you, but the heaviness in my heart felt unrelenting. I was making du'a, I was taking care of myself, I was trusting Allah's wisdom—but I was still waking up every morning with tears.

Yet something beautiful was happening in the midst of all this pain: I was getting closer to Allah. In my raw vulnerability, my conversations with Him became more honest, more frequent, more desperate in the most sacred way. Grief stripped away pretense and brought me to a place of complete dependence on Allah that I had never experienced before.

One day, I made a particularly sincere du'a to Allah. I asked Him simply: "Oh Allah, please make my heart lighter." It wasn't a complicated request or a lengthy supplication. Just a raw, honest plea from someone who was tired of carrying such heavy sadness.

The next morning was the first morning I didn't wake up with tears.

This wasn't the end of my grief journey—healing continued gradually over time. But that morning showed me something profound about Step 7 of our framework: receiving with *shukr* (gratitude). Sometimes what we receive isn't the complete answer we're seeking, but a sign that Allah is responding, that our hearts are slowly healing, that lighter days are possible.

The du'a didn't erase my sadness completely, but it marked the beginning of a different relationship with my grief—one where I could carry my love for my sister without being crushed by the weight of loss.

Months later, as my heart continued to heal, I found myself making Istikhara prayer about a major life decision: leaving my job. The spiritual intimacy that grief had cultivated with Allah gave me the courage to seek His guidance on this transition. Through that prayer process, I felt led to plan my exit and pursue a business that felt more aligned with who I was becoming through this experience of loss and growth.

Looking back now, I realize I was unconsciously implementing the seven-step Islamic manifestation framework long before I had it mapped out. I was asking (du'a), I was taking action (maintaining routines despite difficulty), I was trusting (tawakkul in Allah's wisdom), I was patient when things did move as I had expected, and I was receiving His responses with gratitude—even when those responses came as gradual healing rather than instant relief.

This experience taught me that in seasons of deep sorrow, even small shifts—like one tear-free morning—are gifts worth receiving with profound gratitude. And sometimes, it's in our darkest moments that we discover how much closer we can get to the Light.

## HEALTH CHALLENGES

### WHEN YOUR BODY NEEDS HEALING

Whether facing chronic illness, surgery, or health scares, these seasons test your faith while offering opportunities for spiritual refinement and trust in Allah's decree.

Your Seven-Step Framework:

1. Visualize with Niyyah: Envision yourself healthy and using your restored health to serve Allah better. See yourself as someone who has grown spiritually through this trial.

2. Ask with Du'a: "Ya Allah, You are *Ash-Shafi* (The Healer). Grant me *shifa* (healing) if it's best for me, and if not, grant me *sabr* (patience) and make this illness a source of purification and spiritual elevation."

3. Believe with Yaqeen: Trust that Allah has power over all things, including your health. Believe that whether healing comes through medicine, time, or miracle, it comes from Allah alone.

4. Act with Amal: Seek appropriate medical treatment while maintaining spiritual practices. Eat well, rest, follow medical advice, and continue making du'a. Take care of your body as an *amanah* (trust) from Allah.

5. Trust with Tawakkul: While pursuing treatment, release attachment to specific outcomes. Trust that Allah's decision— whether healing, managing chronic conditions, or other paths— is ultimately best.

6. Surrender with Rida: Accept your current health state while working toward improvement. Find contentment in Allah's decree while still seeking beneficial treatment.

7. Receive with Shukr: Whether you receive the healing you asked for or find strength to live with ongoing challenges, receive whatever comes with gratitude and recognition of Allah's wisdom.

# CAREER CHANGE AND FOLLOWING YOUR PURPOSE

### WHEN ALLAH PLACES A NEW VISION IN YOUR HEART

Sometimes Allah places a calling in your heart that requires significant change—moving from stable but unfulfilling work to something that aligns with your purpose and values.

Your Seven-Step Framework:

1. Visualize with Niyyah: See yourself in work that honors your soul and serves others. Envision the impact you could have and how this change might bring you closer to Allah.

2. Ask with Du'a: "Ya Allah, if this new path is good for my deen, my *dunya* (this world), and my *akhirah* (the next life), make it easy for me. If it's not, redirect my heart toward what's better."

3. Believe with Yaqeen: Trust that Allah has placed this vision in your heart for a reason. Believe that if it's meant for you, Allah will open the necessary doors.

4. Act with Amal: Makes practical preparations—develop new skills, save money for the transition, research your field, and gradually build toward the change while maintaining current responsibilities.

5. Trust with Tawakkul: Move forward with planning while trusting Allah's timing. Don't rush the process or force doors that aren't opening naturally.

6. Surrender with Rida: Be willing to accept if Allah redirects you toward a different path than you initially envisioned. Sometimes our ideas need refinement through divine guidance.

7. **Receive with Shukr:** When opportunities align, recognize them as gifts from Allah. Express gratitude by using your new position to serve others and represent Islam positively.

## REAL STORY OF TRUSTING DIVINE GUIDANCE

The job transition that emerged from my grief journey—the one guided by those Istakhara prayers—happened over fifteen years ago during a challenging economic period. The decision seemed risky to everyone around me: I was quitting my job in a bad economy while still processing the loss of my sister.

What others saw as poor timing, I experienced as divine timing. The spiritual intimacy that grief had cultivated with Allah gave me the clarity to distinguish between His guidance and the world's expectations. My brother Hussein (may Allah be pleased with him) understood this. When I shared my concerns with him, he gave me different counsel than everyone else. He said, "Don't take advice from people who don't share your value system." Then he offered guidance that changed my life: 'Make istikhara, seek Allah's direction, and then follow what you're guided to do.

I applied the seven-step framework to this major life decision. I visualized work that would allow me to practice my faith fully. I made du'a for guidance. I believed Allah would provide. I took the practical step of preparing financially. I trusted His timing. I surrendered my fears about security. And when I received His guidance through istikhara, I followed it.

*Alhamdulillah* (all praise is to Allah), I have been successfully self-employed ever since. That choice revealed a deeper truth: when divine guidance contradicts conventional wisdom, faith requires choosing Allah's path. When you align your choices with divine guidance rather than social expectations, Allah opens doors you never could have imagined.

# ANCHORING YOUR PRACTICE IN SACRED TIME

Beyond major life transitions, Islam offers spiritual rhythms throughout the year to keep you centered in your manifestation practice:

## RAMADAN: THE SEASON OF INTENSIFIED DU'A

- Tap into the *barakah* (blessings) of suhoor and iftar for powerful manifestation
- Let fasting clear emotional and mental blocks
- Share goals and du'a in circles of remembrance
- Make *sadaqah* (voluntary charity) a regular part of your manifestation cycle

## DAILY AND WEEKLY RHYTHMS

- Jumu'ah: Use Friday as your weekly manifestation review
- Last Third of the Night: Sacred window for *tahajjud* (voluntary night prayer) and heartfelt du'a
- Five Daily Prayers: Let each salah reconnect your vision with divine will

## UNIVERSAL PRINCIPLES FOR EVERY SEASON

1. Start with Istighfar: Begin any manifestation practice by seeking forgiveness
2. Include Others: Make du'a for your family, community, and *ummah* (Muslim community) alongside personal goals
3. Maintain Gratitude: Acknowledge current blessings while seeking more
4. Stay Connected: Maintain community relationships for support and accountability
5. Serve Others: Use your blessings and challenges to help others facing similar situations

No matter what season you're in, the seven-step framework provides both spiritual stability and practical guidance— whether you're walking through seasons of plenty or want, joy or sorrow, certainty or doubt or a defining moment in your life.

## SPIRITUAL TAKEAWAY

Every season of life offers unique opportunities for spiritual growth and manifestation. The framework remains constant, but the application adapts to your circumstances. Trust that Allah has lessons for you in every season and that each experience, whether joyful or challenging, can draw you closer to Him.

---

## JOURNEY PROMPTS

1. What season of life are you in right now, and what unique opportunities does it offer for growth?
2. How can you adapt the seven-step framework to your current circumstances?
3. Write about a past difficult season that led to unexpected blessings. What would you tell someone going through something similar?
4. This week, identify one way your current challenge might be preparing you for future blessings. Make du'a for clarity and patience.

---

## AS WE CONTINUE THE JOURNEY

You've learned how to apply Islamic manifestation principles through every season of life, adapting your practice to changing circumstances while maintaining your spiritual center. This resilience is a sign of deep spiritual maturity.

But there's one crucial element we haven't fully addressed: Allah did not intend for you to walk this path alone.

In our final chapter, we'll explore how to build the relationships and community that'll sustain your manifestation journey while honoring your obligations to family and the ummah. Because true abundance doesn't just flow to you—it flows through you to bless others.

## DU'A

*"Ya Allah, guide me through every season of my life with wisdom and grace. Help me see the opportunities for growth in both ease and difficulty. Make every transition a means of drawing closer to You and better serving Your creation."*

"O mankind! We created you from a single (pair) of a male and a female, and made you into nations and tribes, that ye may know each other (not that ye may despise each other)."
(Qur'an 49:13)

# CHAPTER FIFTEEN
## COMMUNITY AND RELATIONSHIPS IN ISLAMIC MANIFESTATION

You don't walk your manifestation journey alone. Islam emphasizes the ummah—the community of believers—as essential to spiritual growth and worldly success. This final chapter explores how to build meaningful relationships that support your goals while honoring your obligations to your family and community.

Understanding this interconnectedness is the first step toward building the support systems that will sustain your manifestation journey. Let's explore how to create intimate circles of spiritual support.

## HOW TO FORM AN ABUNDANCE CIRCLES

### FORMING AN ABUNDANCE CIRCLE: A FAITH-CENTERED GATHERING

While I have not yet formally hosted an "abundance circle," I write from a place of deep experience organizing and facilitating sacred spaces—circles of learning, spiritual reflection, and community growth. What I offer here is inspired by both that history and rooted Islamic traditions of gathering for spiritual alignment.

This model draws upon:

- Islamic principles of *du'a* (supplication) and *tawakkul* (trust in Allah),
- The prophetic tradition of *mutual counsel* (shūra),

- And Sufi practices of communal *dhikr* (remembrance of Allah) and *wazifa* (spiritual recitation gatherings) circles—where participants recite, reflect, and seek divine connection together.

Through my work with Sisters' Steadfast Saturdays and other gatherings, I've seen firsthand the power of collective intention and mutual encouragement. It was through the Sisters' Steadfast Saturdays that I got the inspiration to write this book.

What is an Abundance Circle?

## WHAT ARE ABUNDANCE CIRCLES?

An Abundance Circle is a small group of trusted Muslims who support each other's spiritual and worldly goals through du'a, encouragement, and accountability. Unlike secular mastermind groups that focus solely on business success, Abundance Circles center on Allah in the process and emphasize both *dunya* (this world) and *akhirah* (the next life) goals.

These circles operate on the principle that when believers gather with sincere intentions to support one another's growth, Allah blesses their efforts. As the Prophet (PBUH) said,

> *"The Shaytan is a wolf among mankind just as the wolf is among sheep. He seizes the stray sheep. So beware of the branches (of the main group), and cling to the Jama'ah. Allah's hand is with the Jama'ah."*
> (*Jami' at-Tirmidhi*, Book of Fitan (Book of Trials), Hadith 2166)

We have been warned about being a stray sheep. A collective approach to manifestation multiplies both the spiritual benefits, practical outcomes and the protection from Shaytan.

Now let's explore the core principles of an Abundance Circle

## CORE PRINCIPLES OF ABUNDANCE CIRCLES:

- **Centered on Allah:** All goals and support are filtered through Islamic values
- **Mutual Du'a:** Members regularly pray for each other's success
- **Authentic Sharing:** Safe space to discuss real challenges without judgment
- **Collective Growth:** Everyone's success is celebrated as a blessing from Allah
- **Confidentiality:** What's shared in the circle stays in the circle
- **Service-Oriented:** Goals include serving others and the broader *ummah* (Muslim community)

These principles ensure that your Abundance Circle remains spiritually grounded while providing practical support. Now, let's explore how to create such a circle in your own life.

## HOW TO FORM AN ABUNDANCE CIRCLE

## STEP 1: IDENTIFY POTENTIAL MEMBERS

Look for Muslims who:

- Share your commitment to spiritual growth
- Have goals that align with Islamic principles
- Demonstrate trustworthiness and discretion
- Are supportive rather than competitive
- Balance ambition with humility

The key is finding people who are serious about their spiritual development but also understand the importance of worldly goals when pursued with the right intention. Quality matters more than quantity—even two or three committed members can create a sacred circle.

## STEP 2: SET THE FOUNDATION

Begin your first gathering with:

- Opening du'a for guidance and barakah

- Establishing group norms and confidentiality agreements
- Sharing personal intentions (niyyah) for participating
- Setting meeting frequency (monthly or bi-weekly works well)
- Choosing a rotating leadership structure

This foundational meeting sets the tone for all future gatherings. Take time to ensure everyone understands and commits to the group's purpose and guidelines.

## STEP 3: CREATE YOUR GROUP PRACTICES

Once your foundation is solid, establish consistent practices that will sustain your circle over time:

Monthly Meeting Structure:

- Opening with du'a and gratitude sharing (10 minutes)
- Individual updates on goals and challenges (15 minutes per person)
- Collective problem-solving and advice (20 minutes)
- Specific du'a requests and group du'a (15 minutes)
- Closing with group du'a for the ummah (5 minutes)

Between Meetings:

- Daily du'a for circle members
- Sharing relevant opportunities or resources
- Check-ins during difficult times
- Celebrating each other's wins

This structure ensures that your gatherings remain focused while allowing flexibility for the group's unique needs and dynamics.

## SAMPLE ABUNDANCE CIRCLE GUIDELINES

To help you establish your circle, here's a framework that has proven effective for many groups:

Our Intention (Niyyah): "We gather seeking Allah's pleasure, to support each other's growth in *deen* (religion) and *dunya* (this world), and to use our blessings in service to the ummah."

Our Commitments:
- Maintain strict confidentiality
- Pray regularly for all members
- Share honestly while respecting others' time
- Offer advice with humility and Islamic wisdom
- Celebrate successes and support through challenges
- Include du'a for the broader ummah in our gatherings

Our Boundaries:
- No gossip about people outside the circle
- No pressure to share more than one is comfortable with
- Respect for different levels of Islamic practice
- Focus on solutions and growth, not just complaints
- Balance between worldly and spiritual goals

With your Abundance Circle established, the next step is expanding your du'a practice to encompass your broader relationships.

## DU'A CIRCLES

While Abundance Circles include du'a as part of a broader framework of spiritual growth and goal alignment, a Du'a Circle is more focused in nature. It centers entirely around supplication—coming together to pray for one another with sincerity and trust in Allah. Both are powerful in different ways. Abundance Circles help you align vision with action, while Du'a Circles offer sacred space for pure connection, healing, and barakah through collective prayer.

### THE POWER OF COLLECTIVE DU'A

When you make du'a for others, you invite barakah into your own life. The Prophet (PBUH) said:

> *"When a Muslim makes du'a for his brother in his absence,*
> *the angel says: 'And for you the same.'"*
> (*Sahih Muslim*, The Book of Virtue, Hadith 2588)

This beautiful teaching transforms manifestation into something greater than personal gain—it becomes a web of mutual blessing. Praying for the success, healing, or ease of others doesn't diminish your own possibilities. It expands the spiritual flow for everyone involved.

## EXPANDING YOUR DU'A PRACTICE

One of the most powerful inspirations behind what I now call Family Du'a Time came during a sacred chapter of my life—when my sister was nearing the end of hers. In those tender, final days, I organized prayer circles to surround her with love and du'a. People gathered across time zones and belief systems, united by a shared plea for her ease, mercy, and peace.

That experience showed me the profound healing power of collective supplication. It reminded me that faith isn't meant to be carried alone—and that du'a can connect hearts across any distance.

If you have a supportive family—whether it's your spouse, children, siblings, or chosen kin—consider inviting them into this kind of spiritual practice. Shared du'a strengthens bonds and creates momentum for collective growth and divine alignment.

## IDEAS FOR CREATING FAMILY DU'A TIME:

- Set a weekly gathering for collective du'a
- Let each person share one thing they're praying for
- Make heartfelt du'a for one another's goals and challenges
- Include gratitude for current blessings
- End with du'a for the ummah and for all of humanity

You can include du'as for your spouse, your children, extended family—and yes, even non-Muslim loved ones.

For Spouses: *"Ya Allah, bless our partnership and help us support each other's growth. Make our individual success a means of strengthening our marriage and serving You better."*

For Extended Family: *"Ya Allah, unite our family in righteousness. Let our love, values, and success inspire others toward good."*

For Non-Muslim Family: *"Ya Allah, guide my family to the truth with mercy and light. Open their hearts and draw them near to You."*

## BUILDING BRIDGES THROUGH SHARED GOALS

Sometimes, family members may have different values or struggle to understand your spiritual approach to goal-setting. Rather than creating division, use this as an opportunity to create a connection through shared humanity and universal values:

Focus on Universal Values:

- Health and wellness for the family
- Financial stability and security
- Strong family relationships
- Service to the community

When you frame your goals in terms of these universal values, even family members with different spiritual perspectives can understand and support your efforts.

Include Non-Muslim Family Members: You can make du'a for their guidance while also praying for their worldly success and happiness in ways that honor their dignity. This inclusive approach often opens hearts rather than closing them.

## DEALING WITH SKEPTICAL FAMILY AND FRIENDS

While expanding your du'a practice can bring families together, you may also encounter resistance from those who don't understand or appreciate your approach to Islamic manifestation. This resistance can come from both Muslims and non-Muslims, each presenting unique challenges.

## COMMON CHALLENGES

Understanding the source of skepticism helps you respond with wisdom rather than defensiveness:

"That's Not How Islam Works."
Some Muslims may view goal-setting or visualization as un-Islamic, not understanding the framework you've learned.

Response Strategy:
- Share Qur'anic verses about making du'a with specificity
- Emphasize that you're asking Allah, not the universe
- Point to examples of the Prophet (PBUH) making specific supplications
- Invite them to read relevant chapters of this book

"You're Being Too Worldly."
Others might suggest that focusing on worldly goals contradicts Islamic spirituality.

Response Strategy:
- Explain how your goals serve both *dunya* and *akhirah*
- Share how success can be a means of serving Allah better
- Emphasize your intention to use blessings in charity and service
- Demonstrate through your actions that success hasn't distanced you from Allah

This type of concern often stems from a genuine religious concern, so respond with patience and evidence of your spiritual growth.

"That's Just New Age Stuff."
Some may dismiss Islamic manifestations as repackaged Western concepts.

Response Strategy:
- Point to the long Islamic tradition of du'a, tawakkul, and goal-setting

- Explain that modern manifestation borrowed from Islamic principles - we've been practicing intentional supplication, trust in divine provision, and purposeful action since the time of the Prophet (PBUH)
- Emphasize the differences between Islamic and secular approaches
- Let your spiritual growth speak for itself

Remember that some skepticism stems from protective instincts—people want to guard against innovations in religion. Acknowledge this concern while demonstrating the authentic Islamic foundation of your practice.

## PRACTICAL APPROACHES

Once you understand the source of resistance, you can develop targeted strategies for different relationships.

With Skeptical Family Members:

- Lead by Example: Let your increased spirituality and character speak louder than your words
- Gradual Introduction: Share concepts slowly rather than overwhelming them
- Focus on Shared Values: Emphasize goals that benefit the whole family
- Respect Their Concerns: Listen to their objections with genuine openness
- Maintain Relationships: Don't let differences in goal-setting create distance

The key to a successful family is patience and consistency. They're more likely to be convinced by long-term changes in your character than by theological arguments.

While family requires patience and long-term demonstration, friends often present different opportunities for meaningful dialogue.

With Concerned Friends:

- **Choose Your Audience:** Not everyone needs to know all your goals and methods
- **Emphasize Islamic Foundation:** Always lead with Qur'an and Sunnah references
- **Invite Dialogue:** Be open to their questions and concerns
- **Share Resources:** Offer to share relevant books or articles
- **Pray for Understanding:** Make du'a that Allah opens their hearts to beneficial knowledge

Friends often have more intellectual curiosity than emotional investment, making them potentially more open to reasoned discussion.

However, whether dealing with family concerns or friend questions, the underlying principle remains the same: wisdom lies in discernment.

## SETTING HEALTHY BOUNDARIES

Wisdom lies in knowing what to share with whom. Not every relationship can handle the full depth of your spiritual journey, and that's perfectly acceptable. This discernment extends to practical decisions about the level of detail you share with different people in your life.

What to Share and With Whom:

Inner Circle (Spouse, Supportive Family, Very Close Friends):

- Detailed goals and du'a practices
- Specific challenges and breakthroughs
- Vision board content and journaling insights

Middle Circle (Good Friends, Colleagues/Mentors Who Can Help, Potential Resources):

- General direction of your goals
- Islamic principles you're applying
- Success stories that might inspire them

Outer Circle (Acquaintances, Skeptical/Concerned Relatives):

- Positive changes in your character and spirituality

- General gratitude for Allah's blessings
- Service activities you're involved in

Protective Strategies:

- Don't share vulnerable goals with people who consistently discourage you
- Avoid detailed discussions about methods with those who are philosophically opposed
- Redirect negative conversations toward shared Islamic values
- Remember that not everyone is meant to understand your journey

These boundaries aren't about being secretive—they're about being wise. The Quran demonstrates this wisdom when Prophet Yaqub advised his son Yusuf:

> *"My (dear) little son! relate not thy vision to thy brothers,*
> *lest they concoct a plot against thee: for Satan is to man an*
> *avowed enemy!"*
> (Qur'an 12:5)

Even family members can be influenced by jealousy and Shaytan's whispers. As you become more selective about sharing your journey, you'll naturally seek out communities that can fully support your growth.

You may also have to accept that some people—family, friends, even those you love deeply—may never agree with certain decisions you make. They may not understand your dreams, or they may question your religious approach, your goals, or your methods. And that's okay.

Your ultimate audience is Allah.

He knows your intention. He sees your sincerity. And His approval is what truly matters.

> *"But enough is Allah for a witness."*
> (Qur'an 4:166)

While Allah's approval remains your primary concern, having earthly companions who understand your journey can provide invaluable support and encouragement.

## Finding Like-Minded Muslim Community

When your immediate circle doesn't fully understand your approach to Islamic manifestation, expanding your community becomes essential. The goal is to find Muslims who share your commitment to both spiritual growth and purposeful achievement.

### Where to Look

The key to finding a supportive community is knowing where like-minded Muslims naturally gather.

**Local Masjids and Islamic Centers:**
- Attend programs beyond just Jumu'ah prayer
- Join study circles focused on personal development
- Participate in community service projects
- Attend lectures on spirituality and character development

**Professional and Educational Networks:**
- Muslim professional associations
- Islamic conferences and workshops
- University Muslim student associations (even for non-students)
- Online Islamic learning platforms with local meetups

**Special Interest Groups:**
- Muslim entrepreneurs and business networks
- Islamic personal development workshops
- Muslim women's circles and sisterhood groups
- Islamic coaching and mentorship programs

**Online Communities:**
- Carefully vetted Islamic personal development groups

- Virtual study circles and book clubs
- Islamic coaching and mentorship programs
- Social media groups focused on Islamic lifestyle

While online communities can provide valuable connections, remember to verify the Islamic authenticity of any group before engaging deeply. Look for communities that emphasize the Qur'an and Sunnah alongside personal development.

Once you've identified potential communities, the next step is cultivating meaningful connections within them.

## BUILDING NEW RELATIONSHIPS

Finding the right community is only the first step. Building meaningful relationships within that community requires patience and intentionality.

Starting Conversations About Goals:
Instead of immediately diving into manifestation topics, build relationships around shared Islamic values:

Natural Conversation Starters:
- "What are you most grateful for this year?"
- "How has your faith influenced your career choices?"
- "What Islamic books have impacted you lately?"
- "How do you balance worldly goals with spiritual priorities?"

Deepening Relationships:
- Invite others to Islamic lectures or events
- Start a book club around Islamic personal development texts
- Organize community service projects
- Share meals and build genuine friendships first

Remember that authentic relationships take time to develop and cultivate. Focus on being genuinely interested in others' journeys rather than just finding people who can support yours.

While building personal relationships forms the foundation of community, strategically expanding your professional network amplifies your ability to serve and grow.

## EXPANDING YOUR NETWORK OF SUPPORT

Building Professional Islamic Networks:
Many cities have professional networks for Muslim doctors, lawyers, engineers, teachers, and entrepreneurs. These groups provide:

- Career development and mentorship opportunities
- Business networking with shared Islamic values
- Professional development that honors Islamic principles
- Opportunities to discuss work-life balance from an Islamic perspective

Creating Your Professional Circle:
If formal organizations don't exist in your area:

- Start a monthly coffee meetup for Muslim professionals
- Create a LinkedIn group for Muslims in your industry
- Organize annual iftar gatherings for Muslim colleagues
- Partner with local masjids to host career development workshops

Online Professional Communities:

- Join Islamic business and entrepreneurship groups on social media
- Participate in virtual conferences for Muslim professionals
- Connect with Islamic coaches and mentors
- Engage with Islamic personal development content creators

## MENTORSHIP IN ISLAMIC MANIFESTATION

Finding Mentors: Look for individuals who demonstrate:

- Success in areas where you want to grow
- Strong Islamic character and practice
- Balance between worldly achievement and spiritual development

- Willingness to share knowledge and experience
- Track record of ethical decision-making

Being a Mentor: As you grow in your manifestation journey:

- Share your experiences with those beginning their journey
- Offer practical advice rooted in Islamic principles
- Make du'a for those you mentor
- Connect mentees with opportunities and resources
- Model the integration of faith and ambition

Mentorship Du'a: "Ya Allah, connect me with mentors who will guide me toward what pleases You, and make me a beneficial mentor to those You place in my path."

## COMMUNITY SERVICE AS MANIFESTATION PRACTICE

### THE ISLAMIC PRINCIPLE OF SERVICE

True manifestation in Islam includes using your blessings to serve others. Community service becomes both a form of gratitude and a means of attracting more blessings.

> *"Whoever fulfills the needs of his brother,*
> *Allah will fulfill his needs."*
> (*Sahih al-Bukhari*, Book of Destiny, Hadith 2442)

### INTEGRATING SERVICE WITH PERSONAL GOALS

Professional Skills as Service:

- Offer pro bono work in your field to Islamic organizations
- Mentor young Muslims entering your profession
- Use your expertise to solve community problems
- Teach financial literacy, business skills, or other expertise

**Family Service Projects:**

- Volunteer together at Islamic centers or community organizations
- Adopt a family in need of ongoing support
- Participate in interfaith community service
- Organize neighborhood clean-up or improvement projects

**Using Your Network for Good:**

- Connect job seekers with opportunities
- Introduce potential business partners or collaborators
- Share resources and opportunities with your community
- Advocate for Islamic representation in your professional field

As your manifestation practice bears fruit and Allah blesses your efforts, you'll face new challenges around managing success within your community relationships.

## NAVIGATING SUCCESS IN COMMUNITY

### HANDLING OTHERS' REACTIONS TO YOUR SUCCESS

**When Blessings Come:**

- Share gratitude publicly while keeping specifics private when appropriate
- Use success as an opportunity to help others
- Remain humble and attribute success to Allah
- Increase your charitable giving and community involvement

**Dealing with Envy or Resentment:**

- Continue making du'a for those who might resent your success
- Avoid flaunting blessings in front of those struggling
- Use your platform to lift others up
- Remember that some tests come through blessings, not just hardships

Maintaining Relationships Through Changes:

- Keep the same character regardless of external changes
- Continue investing in relationships even when busy with new opportunities
- Remember those who supported you before success came
- Use increased resources to benefit your community

How we handle success not only affects our own spiritual state but also influences how others perceive the integration of faith and achievement.

## BEING A GOOD EXAMPLE

For Other Muslims:

- Show that success and strong faith can coexist
- Demonstrate Islamic business ethics and character
- Support other Muslims' manifestation journeys
- Share your story in ways that inspire rather than intimidate

For Non-Muslims:

- Let your character reflect the beauty of Islam
- Show that religious people can be ambitious and successful
- Demonstrate Islamic principles through your business and personal interactions
- Use opportunities to educate others about Islamic values

Individual success, when handled with Islamic character, naturally evolves into a desire to create lasting positive impact.

# CREATING LEGACY THROUGH COMMUNITY

## BUILDING GENERATIONAL IMPACT

For Your Community:

- Establish Islamic educational or business programs
- Create scholarships or mentorship opportunities

- Support Islamic institutions and organizations
- Build businesses that provide employment for Muslims

For the Ummah:

- Contribute to the positive representation of Muslims in your field
- Support Islamic causes and organizations globally
- Use your skills and resources to address community challenges
- Mentor the next generation of Muslim leaders

## SPIRITUAL TAKEAWAY

You should not attempt to walk your manifestation journey alone. In Islam, individual success is meaningless unless it benefits the community. Build relationships that honor both your personal growth and your obligations to family and ummah. True abundance flows through connections rooted in mutual support, shared values, and collective elevation.

## JOURNEY PROMPTS

1. Who in your life would be supportive of your Islamic manifestation journey? Who might resist it?
2. How can your personal success become a means of elevating your family and community?
3. Write a plan for creating or joining an Abundance Circle. Include potential members and meeting structure. Remember the circle can be small (2-4) people.
4. This week, share one aspect of your journey with someone you trust.

## AS WE COMPLETE THIS JOURNEY

Community and relationships are the foundation for all sustainable success. As you've learned to create abundance circles, navigate family dynamics, and build networks rooted in Islamic values, you've discovered that your manifestation journey is part of a larger tapestry—connected to your family, your local community, and the global ummah.

The actual test of Islamic manifestation isn't just what you achieve but how your achievements serve Allah's creation and strengthen the bonds of faith and love in your community. When your success becomes a source of inspiration, support, and elevation for others, you know you're walking the path of authentic Islamic abundance.

But this isn't an ending—it's a commencement. You now have the complete framework, the practical tools, and the community understanding to live these principles for the rest of your life. As we close this journey together, let's reflect on where you've been, who you've become, and how Allah might be calling you forward.

## DU'A

*"Ya Allah, surround me with righteous companions who support my growth in both deen and dunya. Help me be a source of encouragement and support for others on their journeys. Unite my family in righteousness and let our successes strengthen our collective bond. Make my achievements a means of serving You and benefiting Your creation. Guide me to build relationships that draw us all closer to You."*

# FINAL REFLECTIONS

You began this book seeking to bring your dreams to life. Hopefully, along the way, you've discovered something far more profound: a path to align your entire life with divine will, to transform your relationship with Allah, and to become someone worthy of the blessings you seek.

This evolution hasn't been accidental. Every chapter, every reflection, every moment of resistance or breakthrough has been preparing you for this moment when you realize that Islamic manifestation was never about getting what you want from Allah.

It was always about becoming who Allah wants you to be.

## WHERE YOUR DU'A BECOMES YOUR DIRECTION.

This book has guided you through a journey—not only of goal-setting and dreaming but of remembrance, realignment, and return. You've asked from the depths of your heart. You've believed with yaqeen. You've acted, trusted, surrendered, and learned to receive. And through it all, you've remembered that Allah is at the center, not the universe, not yourself, not the outcome.

True manifestation in Islam is not about control. It's about connection.

It's not about calling things into existence. It's about calling upon the One who created all existence.

As you continue forward, remember that every breath, every longing, every step can be an act of worship when offered with sincerity. Let your du'a be your compass. Let your trust in Allah be your strength. And let your life reflect the quiet, consistent alignment you've cultivated here.

You don't have to be perfect to be in alignment.

You have to be intentional.

And you never have to walk alone.

## JOURNEY PROMPT

1. What has shifted most profoundly for you—spiritually, emotionally, or practically—through this journey?
2. Which principle from this book do you most need to embody in the coming year?
3. Write a letter to yourself one year from now. Describe who you've become and what you've achieved through aligned manifestation.
4. This week, choose one practice from this entire book to commit to for the next 40 days. Let consistency deepen your transformation.

## DU'A

*"Ya Allah,*
*Let my heart remain close to You.*
*Let my dreams be a reflection of trust, not attachment.*
*Let my actions be rooted in sincerity.*
*Let my striving be lightened by surrender.*
*And let my life be an answered du'a—pleasing to You and aligned with Your wisdom.*
*Ameen."*

# APPENDIX

# THE 99 NAMES OF ALLAH (ASMA'UL HUSNA)

The Most Beautiful Names of Allah, as mentioned in the Qur'an and Hadith, with their meanings:

1. **Ar-Rahman** - The Beneficent
2. **Ar-Rahim** - The Merciful
3. **Al-Malik** - The Eternal Lord
4. **Al-Quddus** - The Most Sacred
5. **As-Salam** - The Embodiment of Peace
6. **Al-Mu'min** - The Infuser of Faith
7. **Al-Muhaymin** - The Preserver of Safety
8. **Al-Aziz** - All Mighty
9. **Al-Jabbar** - The Compeller, The Restorer
10. **Al-Mutakabbir** - The Supreme, The Majestic
11. **Al-Khaliq** - The Creator, The Maker
12. **Al-Bari'** - The Evolver
13. **Al-Musawwir** - The Fashioner
14. **Al-Ghaffar** - The Great Forgiver
15. **Al-Qahhar** - The All-Prevailing One
16. **Al-Wahhab** - The Supreme Bestower
17. **Ar-Razzaq** - The Provider
18. **Al-Fattah** - The Supreme Solver
19. **Al-'Alim** - The All-Knowing
20. **Al-Qabid** - The Withholder
21. **Al-Basit** - The Extender
22. **Al-Khafid** - The Reducer
23. **Ar-Rafi'** - The Exalter, The Elevator

24. **Al-Mu'izz** - The Honourer, The Bestower

25. **Al-Muzill** - The Dishonourer, The Humiliator

26. **As-Sami'** - The All-Hearing

27. **Al-Basir** - The All-Seeing

28. **Al-Hakam** - The Impartial Judge

29. **Al-'Adl** - The Utterly Just

30. **Al-Latif** - The Subtle One, The Most Gentle

31. **Al-Khabir** - The All-Aware

32. **Al-Halim** - The Most Forbearing

33. **Al-'Azim** - The Magnificent, The Supreme

34. **Al-Ghafur** - The Great Forgiver

35. **Ash-Shakur** - The Most Appreciative

36. **Al-'Ali** - The Most High, The Exalted

37. **Al-Kabir** - The Greatest

38. **Al-Hafiz** - The Preserver

39. **Al-Muqit** - The Sustainer

40. **Al-Hasib** - The Reckoner

41. **Al-Jalil** - The Majestic

42. **Al-Karim** - The Most Generous, The Most Esteemed

43. **Ar-Raqib** - The Watchful

44. **Al-Mujib** - The Responsive One

45. **Al-Wasi'** - The All-Encompassing, The Boundless

46. **Al-Hakim** - The All-Wise

47. **Al-Wadud** - The Most Loving

48. **Al-Majid** - The Glorious, The Most Honorable

49. **Al-Ba'ith** - The Infuser of New Life

50. **Ash-Shahid** - The All Observing Witness

51. **Al-Haqq** - The Absolute Truth

52. **Al-Wakil** - The Trustee, The Disposer of Affairs

53. **Al-Qawi** - The All-Strong

54. **Al-Matin** - The Firm, The Steadfast

55. **Al-Wali** - The Protecting Associate

56. **Al-Hamid** - The Praiseworthy

57. **Al-Muhsi** - The All-Enumerating, The Counter

58. **Al-Mubdi'** - The Originator, The Initiator

59. **Al-Mu'id** - The Restorer, The Reinstater

60. **Al-Muhyi** - The Giver of Life

61. **Al-Mumit** - The Inflicter of Death

62. **Al-Hayy** - The Ever-Living

63. **Al-Qayyum** - The Sustainer, The Self-Subsisting

64. **Al-Wajid** - The Perceiver

65. **Al-Majid** - The Illustrious, The Magnificent

66. **Al-Wahid** - The One

67. **Al-Ahad** - The Unique, The Only One

68. **As-Samad** - The Eternal, Satisfier of Needs

69. **Al-Qadir** - The Omnipotent One

70. **Al-Muqtadir** - The Powerful

71. **Al-Muqaddim** - The Expediter, The Promoter

72. **Al-Mu'akhkhir** - The Delayer

73. **Al-Awwal** - The First

74. **Al-Akhir** - The Last

75. **Az-Zahir** - The Manifest

76. **Al-Batin** - The Hidden One, Knower of the Hidden

77. **Al-Wali** - The Governor, The Patron

78. **Al-Muta'ali** - The Self Exalted

79. **Al-Barr** - The Source of All Goodness

80. **At-Tawwab** - The Ever-Pardoning, The Relenting

81. **Al-Muntaqim** - The Avenger

82. **Al-'Afuww** - The Pardoner

83. **Ar-Ra'uf** - The Most Kind

84. **Malik-ul-Mulk** - Master of the Kingdom, Owner of the Dominion

85. **Dhul-Jalali Wal-Ikram** - Possessor of Glory and Honour, Lord of Majesty and Generosity

86. **Al-Muqsit** - The Just One

87. **Al-Jami'** - The Gatherer, The Uniter

88. **Al-Ghani** - The Self-Sufficient, The Wealthy

89. **Al-Mughni** - The Enricher

90. **Al-Mani'** - The Withholder

91. **Ad-Darr** - The Distresser

92. **An-Nafi'** - The Propitious, The Benefactor

93. **An-Nur** - The Light, The Illuminator

94. **Al-Hadi** - The Guide

95. **Al-Badi'** - The Incomparable Originator

96. **Al-Baqi** - The Everlasting

97. **Al-Warith** - The Inheritor, The Heir

98. **Ar-Rashid** - The Guide, Infallible Teacher

99. **As-Sabur** - The Forbearing, The Patient

*Note: These names appear throughout the Qur'an and authentic Hadith. Reflecting on their meanings deepens our understanding of Allah's attributes and helps us call upon Him with knowledge and consciousness.*

# GLOSSARY

**Abd (عبد) [AH-bid]**

Servant or slave of Allah. This term emphasizes the relationship between humans and Allah as Creator and creation, highlighting our role as devoted servants rather than independent beings.

**Akhirah (الآخرة) [AH-khee-rah]**

The Hereafter or Next Life. Refers to the eternal life after death, which Muslims believe is the ultimate destination and more important than this temporary worldly life.

**Akhlaaq (أخلاق) [akh-LAAQ]**

Islamic ethics, morals, or character. Refers to the moral principles and virtues that should guide a Muslim's behavior and interactions with others.

**Al-Ghaib (الغيب) [al-GHAYB]**

The unseen or hidden realm; knowledge that is beyond human perception and belongs exclusively to Allah. This includes knowledge of the future, the afterlife, what is in people's hearts, and other matters that only Allah knows. Seeking knowledge of al-ghaib from sources other than divine revelation is considered shirk in Islam.

**Amal (عمل) [AH-mal]**

Righteous deeds or actions. In Islamic context, it refers to actions performed with good intention and in accordance with Islamic teachings.

Barakah (بركة) [bah-rah-KAH]

Divine blessing that brings increase, growth, and spiritual benefit. Barakah is a special quality that Allah places in people, things, or actions that multiplies their goodness and benefit.

Bismillah (بسم الله) [bis-mil-LAAH]

"In the name of Allah." The phrase Muslims say before beginning any task, acknowledging Allah's guidance and seeking His blessing.

Deen (دين) [DEEN]

Religion or way of life. In Islam, it encompasses all aspects of faith, worship, morality, and conduct as prescribed by Allah.

Dhikr (ذكر) [THIK-er or ZIK-er]

The verbal or mental remembrance of Allah through phrases such as *SubhanAllāh* (glory be to Allah), *Alḥamdulillāh* (all praise is due to Allah), and *Allāhu Akbar* (Allah is the Greatest). Dhikr softens the heart, centers the soul, and draws one closer to divine presence.

Du'a (دعاء) [doo-AH]

The act of supplication or calling upon Allah for help, guidance, or blessings. Du'a is not merely a request—it is a form of worship and connection rooted in trust, humility, and sincerity.

Dunya (دنيا) [DOON-yah]

This worldly life, as opposed to the eternal life of the Hereafter. While not inherently negative, excessive attachment to dunya can distract from spiritual priorities.

Fitrah (فطرة) [FIT-rah]

The natural, innate disposition or God-given nature that inclines humans toward goodness, truth, and worship of Allah.

Halal (حلال) [ha-LAAL]

Permissible or lawful according to Islamic law. Refers to anything that Allah has allowed in terms of actions, food, business practices, etc.

Haram (حرام) [ha-RAAM]

Forbidden or unlawful according to Islamic law. Refers to anything that Allah has prohibited.

Ibadah (عبادة) [ee-bah-DAH]

Worship or acts of devotion to Allah. This includes both ritual worship (like prayer) and everyday actions performed with the intention of pleasing Allah.

Ihsan (إحسان) [ih-SAAN]

Excellence in worship, behavior, and intention. Ihsan is to worship Allah as though you see Him, and even if you do not see Him, knowing that He sees you. It represents the highest spiritual state.

Ikhlas (إخلاص) [ikh-LAAS]

Sincerity, purity of intention, or doing something solely for the sake of Allah—without seeking praise, recognition, or worldly reward.

Iman (إيمان) [ee-MAAN]

Faith or belief in Allah and all aspects of Islamic teaching. Iman includes belief in the heart, declaration with the tongue, and action with the limbs.

Istikhara (استخارة) [is-ti-KHAA-rah]

A specific du'a seeking Allah's guidance for the best outcome in times of uncertainty. It was taught by the Prophet (PBUH) and is used when making important decisions, relying on divine wisdom over personal preference.

Istighfar (استغفار) [is-tigh-FAAR]

Seeking forgiveness from Allah. The act of asking Allah for forgiveness for one's sins and shortcomings.

Jumu'ah (جمعة) [JU-mu-ah]

Friday congregational prayer that is obligatory for Muslim men and recommended for women. It includes a sermon (khutbah) and communal prayer.

Masjid (مسجد) [MAS-jid]

Mosque; a place of worship for Muslims where congregational prayers are held and community gatherings take place.

Niyyah (نية) [nee-YAH]

The conscious, purposeful intention to act for the sake of Allah. Niyyah gives meaning to our actions and aligns them with our spiritual goals. In Islamic practice, every act begins with intention.

Qadr (قدر) [QAH-dar]

Divine decree or predestination. The belief that Allah has knowledge of and control over all that happens, while humans still have free will and responsibility for their choices.

Qiblah (قبلة) [QIB-lah]

The direction Muslims face during prayer, toward the Kaaba in Mecca.

Rabb (رب) [RAB]

A divine name of Allah, referring to the One who creates, sustains, nurtures, and has complete authority over all of creation.

Rahmah (رحمة) [rah-MAH]

Mercy. Rahmah is one of Allah's most emphasized attributes and refers to His boundless compassion, forgiveness, and tenderness.

Rajaa (رجاء) [ra-JAA]

Hope, particularly hope in Allah's mercy and positive expectations of His response to prayers and good deeds.

Rak'ah (ركعة) [rak-AH]

A unit of prayer consisting of standing, bowing, and prostrating. Different prayers consist of different numbers of rak'ahs.

Rida (رضا) [ri-DAA]

Contentment with Allah's decree. Rida is the spiritual state of accepting what Allah has willed, with grace and serenity, even when it differs from our desires.

Rizq (رزق) [RIZQ]

Provision bestowed by Allah. Rizq encompasses material, emotional, spiritual, and intellectual blessings. It includes what is seen and what is hidden, and always comes from divine wisdom.

Sabr (صبر) [SAH-ber]

Patience, perseverance, and steadfastness. Sabr is not passive—it is an active trust in Allah while enduring difficulty or delay without resentment or despair.

Sadaqah (صدقة) [sa-da-QAH]

Voluntary charity given for the sake of Allah. Unlike zakat (obligatory charity), sadaqah can be given at any time and in any amount.

Sakinah (سكينة) [sa-kee-NAH]

Divine tranquility, peace, or serenity that Allah places in the hearts of believers during times of difficulty or spiritual connection.

Salah (صلاة) [sa-LAAH / sa-LAAT]

The formal prayer that Muslims perform five times daily. One of the Five Pillars of Islam.

Salawat (صلوات) [sa-la-WAAT]

Blessings sent upon Prophet Muhammad (PBUH), typically the phrase "Peace and blessings be upon him."

Shifa (شفاء) [shee-FAA]

Healing or cure, particularly divine healing that comes from Allah. While shifa can refer to both physical and spiritual healing, Muslims believe that all true healing ultimately comes from Allah, whether through medicine, natural remedies, or direct divine intervention. Often used in du'a when asking Allah for recovery from illness or spiritual ailments.

Shirk (شرك) [SHIRK]

The sin of associating partners with Allah or attributing divine qualities to anything other than Allah. Considered the gravest sin in Islam.

Shukr (شكر) [SHUKR]

Gratitude. Shukr is acknowledging and appreciating Allah's blessings through words, actions, and heartfelt remembrance.

Sujud (سجود) [su-JOOD]

Prostration, the act of placing one's forehead on the ground in worship. The lowest physical position that represents the highest spiritual state of humility before Allah.

Sunnah (سنة) [SUN-nah]

The teachings, practices, and example of Prophet Muhammad (PBUH). Also refers to recommended (but not obligatory) acts in Islamic law.

Tafakkur (تفكر) [ta-fak-KUR]

Contemplation or deep reflection. Tafakkur allows one to reflect on Allah's signs, purpose, and blessings, serving as a gateway to spiritual clarity and inner wisdom.

Tahajjud (تهجد) [tah-HAJ-jud]

The voluntary night prayer performed after sleeping and before Fajr (dawn prayer), typically in the last third of the night. This sunnah (recommended) prayer is considered one of the most spiritually rewarding acts of worship, when du'a is most likely to be accepted and the connection with Allah is deepest.

Taqwa (تقوى) [TAQ-wa]

God-consciousness or piety. The state of being constantly aware of Allah and striving to obey His commands while avoiding what He has forbidden.

Tarawih (تراويح) [ta-ra-WEEH]

Special voluntary prayers performed during the nights of Ramadan after the regular evening prayer.

Tawaakul (تواكل) [ta-waa-KUL]

False reliance or passivity disguised as trust in Allah. Unlike true tawakkul, tawaakul involves claiming to trust Allah while failing to take appropriate action or effort. It represents a misunderstanding of Islamic trust that leads to inaction rather than the balanced approach of effort combined with surrender.

Tawakkul (توكل) [ta-wak-KUL]

Trust and reliance on Allah. Tawakkul is entrusting one's affairs to Allah while taking all permissible means. It involves effort, surrender, and deep spiritual confidence that what Allah wills is best.

Tawbah (توبة) [TAW-bah]

Repentance; turning back to Allah with regret for sins, seeking forgiveness, and resolving not to repeat the wrongdoing.

Tawheed (توحيد) [taw-HEED]

The belief in the oneness of Allah. Tawheed is the foundational Islamic concept of monotheism—recognizing that Allah is One, without partner, rival, or equal in His essence, attributes, and actions.

Tazkiyah (تزكية) [taz-kee-YAH]

Purification of the soul; the process of spiritual growth and self-development through Islamic practices that cleanse the heart from negative traits and cultivate positive qualities.

Ubudiyyah (عبودية) [u-bu-dee-YAH]

Servitude or worship of Allah. The recognition that humans are created to serve and worship Allah alone.

Ujub (عجب) [U-jub]

Self-conceit or vanity; being impressed with oneself in a way that leads to spiritual pride and forgetfulness of Allah.

Wazifa (وظيفة) [wa-ZEE-fah]

A prescribed spiritual practice or devotional exercise, typically involving repeated dhikr (remembrance of Allah), Qur'anic recitations, or prayers. Often assigned by spiritual guides in Sufi traditions, wazifa practices are designed to bring one closer to Allah and achieve spiritual purification through regular, disciplined recitation.

Wudu (وضوء) [wu-DOO]

Ritual washing performed before prayer to achieve physical and spiritual purity.

Yaqeen (يقين) [ya-QEEN]

Conviction and certainty in Allah. Yaqeen is unwavering belief in His promises, power, and wisdom, even when outcomes are unknown or delayed.

Pronunciation Notes:
- Capital letters indicate stressed syllables

- "AA" represents a long "a" sound (like "father")
- "EE" represents a long "e" sound (like "see")
- "OO" represents a long "u" sound (like "moon")
- The letter "Q" in Arabic is pronounced from deeper in the throat than English "k"
- "KH" is pronounced like the "ch" in German "Bach" or Scottish "loch"
- "TH" can be pronounced as either "th" (like "think") or "z" depending on regional dialect

# Complete Qur'anic References Used in The Book

## Organized by Surah (Chapter) Number

## Surah Al-Fatiha (1)

1:2 - "All praise is due to Allah, Lord of all the worlds." (Ch. 9)

1:5 - "Thee do we worship, and Thine aid we seek." (Ch. 1, 2)

## Surah Al-Baqarah (2)

2:44 - "Do ye enjoin right conduct on the people, and forget (to practise it) yourselves, and yet ye study the Scripture? Will ye not understand?" (Interlude II)

2:168 - "O ye people! Eat of what is on earth, Lawful and good..." (Ch. 10)

2:186 - "When My servants ask thee concerning Me, I am indeed close (to them): I listen to the prayer of every suppliant when he calleth on Me: Let them also, with a will, Listen to My call, and believe in Me: That they may walk in the right way." (Ch. 1, 4, 5)

2:216 - "But it is possible that ye dislike a thing which is good for you; and that ye love a thing which is bad for you. But Allah knoweth, and ye know not." (Ch. 8, 10, 12)

2:219 - "They ask thee concerning wine and gambling. Say: 'In them is great sin, and some profit, for men; but the sin is greater than the profit.'" (Ch. 3)

2:238 - "Guard strictly your (habit of) prayers, especially the Middle Prayer; and stand before Allah in a devout (frame of mind)." (Ch. 12)

2:261 - "The parable of those who spend their substance in the way of Allah is that of a grain of corn: it groweth seven ears, and each ear Hath a hundred grains. Allah giveth manifold increase to whom He pleaseth: And Allah careth for all and He knoweth all things." (Ch. 5)

2:268 - "The Evil one threatens you with poverty and bids you to conduct unseemly. Allah promiseth you His forgiveness and bounties. And Allah careth for all and He knoweth all things." (Ch. 5)

2:286 - "On no soul doth Allah Place a burden greater than it can bear. It gets every good that it earns, and it suffers every ill that it earns. " (Part One)

## SURAH AL-IMRAN (3)

3:8 - "Our Lord! (they say), Let not our hearts deviate now after Thou hast guided us, but grant us mercy from Thine own Presence; for Thou art the Grantor of bounties without measure." (Part Two)

3:103 - "And hold fast, all together, by the rope which Allah (stretches out for you), and be not divided among yourselves." (Ch. 10)

3:159 - "It is part of the Mercy of Allah that thou dost deal gently with them Wert thou severe or harsh-hearted, they would have broken away from about thee: so pass over (Their faults), and ask for (Allah's) forgiveness for them; and consult them in affairs (of moment). Then, when thou hast Taken a decision trust in Allah. For Allah loves those who put their trust (in Him)." (Ch. 7)

3:173 - "For us Allah sufficeth, and He is the best disposer of affairs." (Ch. 2)

3:190-191 - "Behold! in the creation of the heavens and the earth, and the alternation of night and day,- there are indeed Signs for men of understanding,- Men who celebrate the praises of Allah, standing, sitting, and lying down on their sides, and contemplate the (wonders of) creation in the heavens and the earth, (With the thought): 'Our Lord! not for naught Hast Thou created (all) this! Glory to Thee! Give us salvation from the penalty of the Fire.'" (Ch. 4)

## Surah An-Nisa (4)

4:135 - "O ye who believe! Stand out firmly for justice, as witnesses to Allah, even as against yourselves, or your parents, or your kin." (Part Three)

4:166 - "But enough is Allah for a witness." (Ch. 15)

## Surah Al-A'raf (7)

7:156 - "...but my mercy extendeth to all things." (Ch. 5)

7:205 - "And do thou (O reader!) Bring thy Lord to remembrance in thy (very) soul, with humility and in reverence, without loudness in words, in the mornings and evenings; and be not thou of those who are unheedful." (Ch. 11)

## Surah Al-Anfal (8)

8:30 - "They plot and plan, and Allah too plans; but the best of planners is Allah." (Ch. 2, 3)

## Surah At-Tawbah (9)

9:129 - "Allah sufficeth me: there is no god but He: On Him is my trust,- He the Lord of the Throne (of Glory) Supreme!" (Appendix)

## Surah Yunus (10)

10:3 - "Verily your Lord is Allah, who created the heavens and the earth in six days, and is firmly established on the throne (of authority), regulating and governing all things." (Ch. 3)

## Surah Hud (11)

11:6 - "There is no moving creature on earth but its sustenance dependeth on Allah: He knoweth the time and place of its definitive abode and its temporary deposit: All is in a clear Record." (Ch. 1)

11:37-38 - References to Prophet Nuh (AS) building the ark (Ch. 7)

11:61 - "Indeed, your Lord is near and responsive." (Ch. 6)

## SURAH YUSUF (12)

12:5 - "My (dear) little son! relate not thy vision to thy brothers, lest they concoct a plot against thee: for Satan is to man an avowed enemy!" (Ch. 15)

## SURAH AR-RA'D (13)

13:11 - "Allah does not change a people's lot unless they change what is in their hearts." (Ch. 7, 11)

13:28 - "Those who believe, and whose hearts find satisfaction in the remembrance of Allah: for without doubt in the remembrance of Allah do hearts find satisfaction." (Ch. 11)

## SURAH IBRAHIM (14)

14:7 - "And remember! your Lord caused to be declared (publicly): 'If ye are grateful, I will add more (favours) unto you...'" (Introduction, Ch. 1, 8, 9)

14:34 - "And He giveth you of all that ye ask for. But if ye count the favours of Allah, never will ye be able to number them." (Ch. 1)

## SURAH AN-NAHL (16)

16:53 - "And ye have no good thing but is from Allah" (Ch. 1, 4, 9, 10)

16:90 - "Allah commands justice, the doing of good, and liberality to kith and kin, and He forbids all shameful deeds, and injustice and rebellion: He instructs you, that ye may receive admonition." (Ch. 10)

## SURAH AL-ISRA (17)

17:30 - "Verily thy Lord doth provide sustenance in abundance for whom He pleaseth, and He provideth in a just measure. For He doth know and regard all His servants." (Ch. 5)

## SURAH MARYAM (19)

19:25-26 - References to Maryam (AS) shaking the palm tree (Ch. 7)

## SURAH AN-NAML (27)

27:65 - "Say: None in the heavens or on earth, except Allah, knows what is hidden." (Ch. 3)

## SURAH AL-QASAS (28)

28:77 - "But seek, with the (wealth) which Allah has bestowed on thee, the Home of the Hereafter, nor forget thy portion in this world..." (Part Three)

## SURAH AL-ANKABUT (29)

29:45 - "And establish regular prayer: for prayer restrains from shameful and unjust deeds..." (Appendix)

29:64 - "What is the life of this world but amusement and play? but verily the Home in the Hereafter,- that is life indeed, if they but knew." (Ch. 2)

## SURAH LUQMAN (31)

31:22 - "Whoever submits his whole self to Allah, and is a doer of good, has grasped indeed the most trustworthy hand-hold: and with Allah rests the End and Decision of (all) affairs." (Ch. 7, 8)

## SURAH AL-AHZAB (33)

33:3 - "And put thy trust in Allah, and enough is Allah as a disposer of affairs." (Ch. 8)

33:41-42 - "O ye who believe! Celebrate the praises of Allah, and do this often; And glorify Him morning and evening." (Ch. 14)

## SURAH SABA (34)

34:39 - "Say: 'Verily my Lord enlarges and restricts the Sustenance to such of his servants as He pleases: and nothing do ye spend in the least (in His cause) but He replaces it: for He is the Best of those who grant Sustenance.'" (Ch. 1)

## SURAH GHAFIR (40)

40:60 - "And your Lord says, 'Call upon Me; I will respond to you.'" (Ch. 4, 5, 13)

## SURAH MUHAMMAD (47)

47:31 - "And We shall try you until We test those among you who strive their utmost and persevere in patience; and We shall try your reported (mettle)." (Ch. 12)

## SURAH AL-HUJURAT (49)

49:13 - "O mankind! We created you from a single (pair) of a male and a female, and made you into nations and tribes, that ye may know each other (not that ye may despise each other)." (Ch. 14)

## SURAH QAF (50)

50:16 - "We are nearer to him than (his) jugular vein." (Ch. 4)

## SURAH ADH-DHARIYAT (51)

51:22 - "And in heaven is your Sustenance, as (also) that which ye are promised." (Ch. 5)
51:58 - "For Allah is He Who gives (all) Sustenance,- Lord of Power,- Steadfast (for ever)." (Appendix)

## SURAH AN-NAJM (53)

53:39 - "And that there is nothing for man except what he strives for." (Ch. 7)

## SURAH AL-HADID (57)

57:20 - "Know ye (all), that the life of this world is but play and amusement, pomp and mutual boasting and multiplying, (in rivalry) among yourselves, riches and children. Here is a similitude: How rain and the growth which it brings forth, delight (the hearts of) the tillers;

soon it withers; thou wilt see it grow yellow; then it becomes dry and crumbles away. But in the Hereafter is a Penalty severe (for the devotees of wrong). And Forgiveness from Allah and (His) Good Pleasure (for the devotees of Allah). And what is the life of this world, but goods and chattels of deception?" (Ch. 10)

## SURAH AT-TAGHABUN (64)

64:11 - "No kind of calamity can occur, except by the leave of Allah: and if anyone believes in Allah, (Allah) guides his heart (aright): for Allah knows all things." (Ch. 8)

## SURAH AT-TALAQ (65)

65:2-3 - "And for those who fear Allah, He (ever) prepares a way out, And He provides for him from (sources) he never could imagine." (Introduction, Ch. 1, 5)

65:3 - "And if any one puts his trust in Allah, sufficient is (Allah) for him. For Allah will surely accomplish his purpose: verily, for all things has Allah appointed a due proportion." (Part Two, Ch. 5, 10)

## SURAH NUH (71)

71:10-12 - "Saying, 'Ask forgiveness from your Lord; for He is Oft-Forgiving; He will send rain to you in abundance; Give you increase in wealth and sons; and bestow on you gardens and bestow on you rivers (of flowing water).'" (Ch. 5)

## SURAH ASH-SHARH (94)

94:6 - "Verily, with every difficulty there is relief." (Appendix)

## SURAH AL-BAYYINAH (98)

98:5 - "And they have been commanded no more than this: To worship Allah, offering Him sincere devotion, being true (in faith); to establish regular prayer; and to practice regular charity; and that is the Religion Right and Straight." (Ch. 1, 10)

# Qur'an Quick Reference: Key Verses for Daily Practice

## For Morning Intentions:

"Thee do we worship, and Thine aid we seek." (1:5) (Ch. 1, 2)

## For Trust During Uncertainty:

"For us Allah sufficeth, and He is the best disposer of affairs." (3:173) (Ch. 2)
"Then, when thou hast Taken a decision trust in Allah. For Allah loves those who put their trust (in Him)." (3:159) (Ch. 7)

## For Gratitude Practice:

"If ye are grateful, I will add more (favours) unto you." (14:7) (Introduction, Ch. 1, 9)
"And ye have no good thing but is from Allah" (16:53) (Ch. 1, 9)

## For Making Du'a:

"Call on Me; I will answer your (Prayer)." (40:60) (Ch. 5, 13)
"When My servants ask thee concerning Me, I am indeed close (to them): I listen to the prayer of every suppliant when he calleth on Me." (2:186) (Ch. 1, 5)

## For Difficult Times:

"Verily, with every difficulty there is relief." (94:6) (Appendix)
"But it is possible that ye dislike a thing which is good for you, and that ye love a thing which is bad for you. But Allah knoweth, and ye know not." (2:216) (Ch. 8, 10)

FOR TAKING ACTION:

"Allah does not change a people's lot unless they change what is in their hearts" (13:11) (Ch. 7, 11)

*Note: These are translations from Abdullah Yusuf Ali's "The Holy Qur'an: Text, Translation and Commentary." For readers seeking Arabic text, please refer to a complete Qur'an or reliable online resource such as Quran.com.*

# Qur'anic References by Theme

## Wisdom and Discretion

12:5 -"My (dear) little son! relate not thy vision to thy brothers, lest they concoct a plot against thee: for Satan is to man an avowed enemy!" (Ch. 15)

## Du'a and Divine Response

1:5 - "Thee do we worship, and Thine aid we seek." (Ch. 1, 2)

2:186 - "When My servants ask thee concerning Me, I am indeed close (to them): I listen to the prayer of every suppliant when he calleth on Me..." (Ch. 1, 5)

40:60 - "Call on Me; I will answer your (Prayer)..." (Ch. 5, 13)

## Taking Action and Effort

53:39 - "And that there is nothing for man except what he strives for." (Ch. 7)

## Provision and Sustenance

2:261 - "The parable of those who spend their substance in the way of Allah is that of a grain of corn..." (Ch. 5)

11:6 - "There is no moving creature on earth but its sustenance dependeth on Allah..." (Ch. 1)

16:53 - "And ye have no good thing but is from Allah" (Ch. 1, 9)

17:30 - "Verily thy Lord doth provide sustenance in abundance for whom He pleaseth..." (Ch. 5)

34:39 - "Say: 'Verily my Lord enlarges and restricts the Sustenance to such of his servants as He pleases..." (Ch. 1)

51:22 - "And in heaven is your Sustenance, as (also) that which ye are promised." (Ch. 5)

65:2-3 - "And whoever is mindful of Allah, He will make a way out for them, and provide for them from sources they could never imagine." (Introduction, Ch. 1, 5)

71:10-12 - "Saying, 'Ask forgiveness from your Lord; for He is Oft-Forgiving; He will send rain to you in abundance..." (Ch. 5)

## TRUST AND RELIANCE (TAWAKKUL)

3:159 - "Then, when thou hast Taken a decision trust in Allah. For Allah loves those who put their trust (in Him)." (Ch. 7)

3:173 - "For us Allah sufficeth, and He is the best disposer of affairs." (Ch. 2)

31:22 - "Whoever submits his whole self to Allah, and is a doer of good, has grasped indeed the most trustworthy hand-hold..." (Ch. 7, 8)

33:3 - "And put thy trust in Allah, and enough is Allah as a disposer of affairs" (Ch. 8)

65:3 - "And if any one puts his trust in Allah, sufficient is (Allah) for him. For Allah will surely accomplish his purpose: verily, for all things has Allah appointed a due proportion." (Part Two)

## DIVINE WISDOM AND PLANNING

2:216 - "But it is possible that ye dislike a thing which is good for you..." (Ch. 8, 10)

8:30 - "They plot and plan, and Allah too plans; but the best of planners is Allah." (Ch. 3)

11:61 - "Indeed, your Lord is near and responsive." (Ch. 6)

13:11 - "Allah does not change a people's lot unless they change what is in their hearts." (Ch. 7, 11)

27:65 - "Say: None in the heavens or on earth, except Allah, knows what is hidden." (Ch. 3)

64:11 - "No kind of calamity can occur, except by the leave of Allah..." (Ch. 8)

## CONTEMPLATION AND REFLECTION

3:190-191 - "Behold! in the creation of the heavens and the earth, and the alternation of night and day..." (Ch. 4)

13:28 - "Those who believe, and whose hearts find satisfaction in the remembrance of Allah: for without doubt in the remembrance of Allah do hearts find satisfaction." (Ch. 11)

50:16 - "We are nearer to him than (his) jugular vein." (Ch. 4)

## GRATITUDE AND INCREASE

14:7 - "If ye are grateful, I will add more (favours) unto you..." (Introduction, Ch. 1, 9)

## GUIDANCE AND RIGHT PATH

2:44 - "Do ye enjoin right conduct on the people, and forget (to practice it) yourselves, and yet ye study the Scripture? Will ye not understand?" (Interlude II)

3:8 - "Our Lord! (they say), Let not our hearts deviate now after Thou hast guided us, but grant us mercy from Thine own Presence; for Thou art the Grantor of bounties without measure." (Ch. 4)

3:103 - "And hold fast, all together, by the rope which Allah (stretches out for you), and be not divided among yourselves." them in affairs (of moment). Then, when thou hast taken a decision trust in Allah." (Ch. 12)

3:159 - "And consult them in affairs (of moment). Then, when thou hast taken a decision trust in Allah." (Ch. 12)

6:153 - "Verily, this is My way, leading straight: follow it: follow not (other) paths..." (Ch. 2)

98:5 - "And they have been commanded no more than this: To worship Allah, offering Him sincere devotion..." (Ch. 2, 12)

## Prayer and Worship

29:45 - "And establish regular prayer: for prayer restrains from shameful and unjust deeds..." (Ch. 5)

33:41-42 - "O ye who believe! Celebrate the praises of Allah, and do this often; And glorify Him morning and evening." (Ch. 14)

## Integrity and Excellence

4:135 - "O ye who believe! Stand out firmly for justice, as witnesses to Allah..." (Part Three)

16:90 - "Allah commands justice, the doing of good, and liberality to kith and kin, and He forbids all shameful deeds, and injustice and rebellion: He instructs you, that ye may receive admonition." (Ch. 10)

## Testing and Trials

47:31 - "And We shall try you until We test those among you who strive their utmost..." (Ch. 14)

## Community and Unity

49:13 - "O mankind! We created you from a single (pair) of a male and a female, and made you into nations and tribes..." (Ch. 15)

## Overcoming Spiritual Challenges

2:268 - "The Evil one threatens you with poverty and bids you to conduct unseemly..." (Ch. 5)

## Permissible Actions and Guidelines

2:168 - "O ye people! Eat of what is on earth, Lawful and good..." (Ch. 10, 12)

## Allah's Control Over the Universe

7:156 - "But My mercy extendeth to all things..." (Ch. 5)

10:3 - "Verily your Lord is Allah, who created the heavens and the earth in six days, and is firmly established on the throne (of authority), regulating and governing all things." (Ch. 3)

## BALANCE BETWEEN DUNYA AND AKHIRAH

28:77 - "But seek, with the (wealth) which Allah has bestowed on thee, the Home of the Hereafter, nor forget thy portion in this world. " (Part Three)

*Note: These are translations from Abdullah Yusuf Ali's "The Holy Qur'an: Text, Translation and Commentary." For readers seeking Arabic text, please refer to a complete Qur'an or reliable online resource such as Quran.com.*

# Qur'anic Affirmations

## How to Use These Affirmations

**Daily Practice:**
- Choose 3-5 affirmations that resonate with your current needs
- Recite them during morning and evening routines
- Reflect on their meanings rather than just repeating words
- Combine with dhikr and regular prayer

**Specific Situations:**
- Before important decisions: Use guidance and wisdom affirmations
- During difficulty: Focus on ease, relief, and strength affirmations
- When feeling anxious: Emphasize trust, protection, and peace affirmations
- During gratitude practice: Use provision and increase affirmations

**Integration with Manifestation Practice:**
- Use relevant affirmations before making du'a
- Include them in your vision board or journaling practice
- Repeat them during visualization exercises
- Let them shape your mindset throughout the day

**Remember:**
- These are not magic formulas but reminders of Qur'anic truths
- Combine with action, not just passive repetition
- Maintain awareness that Allah's wisdom supersedes your desires
- Use them to strengthen yaqeen (certainty) and tawakkul (trust in Allah)

## For Trust and Reliance (Tawakkul)

"I place my trust in Allah. Surely, Allah loves those who trust Him." (Qur'an 3:159)

"Allah sufficeth me: there is no god but He: On Him is my trust,- He the Lord of the Throne (of Glory) Supreme!" (Qur'an 3:173)

"My Lord is sufficient for me, there is no deity except Him. I place my trust in Him." (Qur'an 9:129)

"And put your trust in Allah; and sufficient is Allah as a disposer of affairs." (Qur'an 33:3)

"And if any one puts his trust in Allah, sufficient is (Allah) for him. For Allah will surely accomplish his purpose: verily, for all things has Allah appointed a due proportion." (Qur'an 65:3)

## For Divine Response and Closeness

"Indeed I am near. I respond to the invocation of the supplicant when he calls upon Me." (Qur'an 2:186)

"Indeed, your Lord is near and responsive." (Qur'an 11:61)

"Call upon Me, I will respond to you." (Qur'an 40:60)

"We are closer to him than his jugular vein." (Qur'an 50:16)

## For Ease and Relief

"On no soul doth Allah Place a burden greater than it can bear." (Qur'an 2:286)

"And whoever fears Allah—He will make for him a way out." (Qur'an 65:2)

"And Allah will surely make for the believers a way out." (Based on Qur'an 65:2-3)

"Indeed, with hardship comes ease." (Qur'an 94:6)

## For Provision and Sustenance

"And whatever blessing I have—it is from Allah." (Qur'an 16:53)

"My Lord extends provision for whom He wills and restricts it, and He is ever Acquainted and Seeing." (Based on Qur'an 17:30)

"In heaven is my provision and whatever I am promised." (Qur'an 51:22)

"For Allah is He Who gives (all) Sustenance,- Lord of Power,- Steadfast (for ever)." (Qur'an 51:58)

## FOR GRATITUDE AND INCREASE

"All praise is due to Allah, Lord of all the worlds." (Qur'an 1:2)

"Those who believe, and whose hearts find satisfaction in the remembrance of Allah..." (Qur'an 13:28)

"If I am grateful, Allah will surely increase me." (Qur'an 14:7)

"I remember Allah, and He remembers me." (Based on Hadith Qudsi in Bukhari)

## FOR DIVINE WISDOM AND ACCEPTANCE

"Allah knows, while I know not." (Qur'an 2:216)

"Allah is the best of planners." (Qur'an 8:30)

"Whatever Allah wills will be, and whatever He does not will, will not be." (Based on Islamic principle)

"I am content with Allah as my Lord, Islam as my religion, and Muhammad as my messenger." (Based on prophetic du'a)

## FOR GUIDANCE AND DIRECTION

"My Lord guides me to the straight path." (Based on Qur'an 6:161)

"Allah guides my heart aright." (Based on Qur'an 64:11)

"I seek Allah's guidance in all my affairs." (Based on Istikhara principle)

"Allah will guide me to what is best for me." (Based on Qur'anic guidance principles)

## FOR STRENGTH AND PATIENCE

"I can bear this, for Allah does not burden a soul beyond its capacity." (Qur'an 2:286)

"With Allah's help, I am strong." (Based on Qur'anic principles)
"I seek strength through Allah alone." (Based on Islamic teachings)

## FOR PROTECTION AND PEACE

"Allah protects me from all that would harm me." (Based on Qur'anic protection verses)
"In Allah I find my peace and security." (Based on Qur'anic teachings)
"No harm can reach me except what Allah has written for me." (Based on prophetic teachings)
"Allah is my protector and my guide." (Based on Qur'anic teachings)

## FOR FORGIVENESS AND MERCY

"Allah's mercy encompasses all things, including me." (Based on Qur'an 7:156)
"Allah is Oft-Forgiving, Most Merciful to me." (Based on multiple Qur'anic verses)
"I turn to Allah in repentance, and He accepts my repentance." (Based on Qur'anic teachings)
"Allah's forgiveness is greater than any sin I could commit." (Based on Islamic teachings)

## FOR SUCCESS AND ACHIEVEMENT

"Allah will complete His favor upon me." (Based on Qur'an 5:3)
"What Allah has written for me will reach me." (Based on prophetic teachings)
"Allah makes all my affairs easy for me." (Based on du'a traditions)
"I work with my hands and trust with my heart." (Based on tawakkul principles)

## FOR SPIRITUAL GROWTH

"My worship and life are for Allah alone." (Based on Qur'an 6:162)
"Allah increases me in faith and certainty." (Based on Qur'anic teachings)

"Every day, Allah draws me closer to Him." (Based on spiritual development principles)

"Allah purifies my heart and guides my actions." (Based on Islamic spiritual goals)

*Note: Affirmations marked "Based on" are derived from Qur'anic principles and Islamic teachings, adapted into first person for personal reflection. Direct quotes maintain the original Qur'anic language.*

# Complete List of Hadith References Used in The Book

## From Sahih al-Bukhari:

- "Allah says: 'I am as My servant thinks I am. I am with him when he remembers Me. If he remembers Me to himself, I remember him to Myself; and if he remembers Me in an assembly, I remember him in an assembly better than it...'" (*Sahih al-Bukhari*, Book of Tawhid, Hadith 7405, Also in: *Sahih Muslim*, Book of Dhikr, Hadith 2675) (Introduction)

- "Truly in the body there is a morsel of flesh which, if it is sound, the whole body is sound; and if it is corrupt, the whole body is corrupt. Truly, it is the heart." (*Sahih al-Bukhari*, Book of Belief, Hadith 52, Also in: *Sahih Muslim*, Book of Governance, Hadith 1599) (Ch. 5, 11)

- "Wealth is not in having many possessions. Rather, true wealth is contentment of the soul." (*Sahih al-Bukhari*, Book of Manners, Hadith 644, Also recorded in *Sahih Muslim*, Hadith 1051) (Ch. 5)

- "A man who travels long distances, disheveled and dusty, raises his hands to the sky saying, 'O Lord, O Lord,' while his food is unlawful, his drink is unlawful, his clothing is unlawful, and he is nourished with the unlawful—so how can his supplication be accepted?" (*Sahih al-Bukhari*, Book of Belief, Hadith 52, *Sahih Muslim*, Book of Governance, Hadith 1599) (Ch. 5)

- "A person's supplication will be accepted so long as he does not become impatient and say, 'I supplicated but it was not accepted.'" (*Sahih al-Bukhari*, Book of Da'awat, Hadith 6340, Also in: *Sahih Muslim*, Book of Dhikr, Hadith 2735) (Ch. 6)

- "The most beloved deeds to Allah are those that are consistent, even if small." (*Sahih al-Bukhari*, Book of Riqaq, Hadith 6464, Also in: *Sahih Muslim*, Book of Salat al-Musafirin, Hadith 782) (Ch. 12)

- "When one of you is concerned about a matter, let him pray two rak'ahs of voluntary prayer, then say: 'O Allah, I seek Your guidance through Your knowledge, and I seek ability through Your power, and I ask You of Your great bounty. You have power; I have none. And You know; I know not. You are the Knower of hidden things. O Allah, if in Your knowledge this matter is good for my religion, my livelihood and my affairs, immediate and in the future, then ordain it for me, make it easy for me, and bless it for me. And if in Your knowledge it is bad for my religion, my livelihood and my affairs, immediate and in the future, then turn it away from me, and turn me away from it. And ordain for me the good wherever it may be, and make me pleased with it.'" (*Sahih al-Bukhari*, Book of Tahajjud, Hadith 1162) (Ch. 10)

- "Whoever fulfills the needs of his brother, Allah will fulfill his needs." (*Sahih al-Bukhari*, Book of Destiny, Hadith 2442) (Ch. 15)

## FROM SAHIH MUSLIM:

- "When a Muslim or a believer washes his face in wudu', every sin he committed with his eyes is washed away... when he washes his hands, every sin they handled is washed away... until he emerges purified from sin." (*Sahih Muslim*, Book of Purification, Hadith 244) (Ch. 5)

- "The closest that a servant comes to his Lord is when he is prostrating, so make plenty of supplication then." (*Sahih Muslim*, Book of Prayer, Hadith 482, Narrated by Abu Huraira (RA)) (Ch. 9)

- "Allah is pleased with the servant who, when he eats something, praises Him, and when he drinks something, praises Him." (*Sahih Muslim*, The Book of Drinks, Hadith 2734, Narrated by Anas ibn Malik (RA)) (Ch. 9)

- "Charity does not decrease wealth." (*Sahih Muslim*, Book 45 (The Book of Virtue, Good Manners, and Joining the Ties of Kinship), Hadith 2588) (Ch. 5)

- "When a Muslim makes du'a for his brother in his absence, the angel says: 'And for you the same.'" (*Sahih Muslim*, The Book of Virtue, Hadith 2588) (Ch. 15)

- "Strive for that which will benefit you, seek the help of Allah, and do not feel helpless." (*Sahih Muslim*, Book of Destiny, Hadith 2664) (Ch. 7)

- "Amazing is the affair of the believer. Verily, all of his affairs are good. If something good happens, he is grateful, and that is good for him. If something bad happens, he is patient, and that is good for him." (*Sahih Muslim*, Book of Zuhd, Hadith 2999) (Ch. 8)

## FROM JAMI' AT-TIRMIDHI:

- "If you were to rely upon Allah with the reliance He is due, you would be given provision like the birds: They go out empty stomachs in the morning and return full at dusk." (*Jami' at-Tirmidhi*, Book of Zuhd, Hadith 2344) (Ch. 1, 5, 8)

- A man said, "O Messenger of Allah, should I tie my camel and trust in Allah, or should I leave her untied and trust in Allah?" The Prophet (PBUH) replied: "Tie her and trust in Allah." (*Jami' at-Tirmidhi*, Book of Sifat al-Qiyamah, Hadith 2517) (Introduction, Ch. 7)

- "Leave that which makes you doubt for that which does not make you doubt. Truth brings peace, and lies bring doubt." (*Jami' at-Tirmidhi*, Book of Righteousness and Maintaining Good Relations, Hadith 2518) (Ch. 10)

- "Du'a is worship." (*Jami' at-Tirmidhi*, Book of Supplications, Hadith 3372) (Ch. 2, 5)
- "Call upon Allah while being certain of being answered." (*Jami' at-Tirmidhi*, Book of Supplications, Hadith 3479) (Ch. 4, 5)
- "Your Lord is munificent and generous and is ashamed to turn away empty the hands of His servant when he raises them to Him." (*Jami' at-Tirmidhi*, Book of Supplications, Hadith 3556) (Ch. 5)
- "The Shaytan is a wolf among mankind just as the wolf is among sheep. He seizes the stray sheep. So beware of the branches (of the main group), and cling to the Jama'ah. Allah's hand is with the Jama'ah." (*Jami' at-Tirmidhi*, Book of Fitan (Book of Trials), Hadith 2166) (Ch. 15)

## FROM SUNAN ABU DAWOOD:

- "Your Lord is munificent and generous and is ashamed to turn away empty the hands of His servant when he raises them to Him." (*Sunan Abi Dawud* 1488, Book 8, Hadith 73) (Ch. 5)

## FROM SUNAN IBN MAJAH:

- "No soul will die until it has received all its provision..." (*Sunan Ibn Majah*, Book of Zuhd, Hadith 2144) (Ch. 5)
- "Take up good deeds only as much as you are able, for the best of deeds is that which is done consistently even if it is small." (*Sunan Ibn Majah*, Book of Zuhd, Hadith 4240) (Ch. 12)

## COMPANION NARRATIONS:

- The Story of Abdullah ibn Mas'ud: A man came to visit Abdullah ibn Mas'ud after having been away for a while. Ibn Mas'ud asked how he was doing, and the man replied that he and his family were well, but financially, he had lost everything. Ibn Mas'ud lowered his head and remained silent for a long time. Then he raised his head and said, "Bring the Holy Qur'an!" He flipped through it until he came to the verse: "Whoever constantly seeks forgiveness, Allah will create a path out of every difficulty, remove every worry, and grant them sustenance from sources they could never imagine." (Qur'an 65:2-3) Ibn Mas'ud then said to the man, "I will give you the same advice that Allah gave you. Constantly seek forgiveness from Allah, and improve your relationship with Him!" (Ch. 5)

*Note: The hadith (prophetic traditions) referenced in this book are primarily drawn from the major authentic collections. For readers interested in further study or verification, consult Sunnah.com or qualified Islamic scholars.*

# Du'as For Practical Use

## How to Use These Du'as

**Daily Practice:**

- Choose 2-3 du'as to focus on each week
- Memorize them gradually in Arabic if possible
- Understand their meanings deeply
- Use them during your morning and evening routines

**Specific Situations:**

- Keep a du'a journal with relevant supplications for different circumstances
- Refer to this collection during your manifestation practice
- Combine personal du'as with these classical ones

**Remember:**

- Du'a can be made in any language, but learning Arabic versions connects you to the prophetic tradition
- Sincerity (ikhlas) is more important than perfect pronunciation
- Make du'a a conversation with Allah, not just recitation

# COMPLETE LIST OF DU'AS (SUPPLICATIONS) REFERENCES USED IN THE BOOK

## FOR GUIDANCE AND CLARITY

*"Ya Allah, guide me to understand the true nature of manifestation through Your divine wisdom. Help me distinguish between what draws me closer to You and what takes me away."* (Ch. 1)

*"Ya Allah, purify my intentions and help me see with the light of sincerity. Align my vision with Your will, and let my dreams serve Your purpose for my life."* (Ch. 4)

*"Ya Allah, place me exactly where You want me. Surround me with people and provision that support the purpose You created me for. Let my joy be a reflection of Your mercy, and let my success draw me nearer to You."* (Ch. 4)

## FOR TRUST AND RELIANCE

*"Ya Allah, teach me to trust You completely. Help me release control and find peace in Your timing. Grant me rida and sabr."* (Ch. 8)

*"O Allah, place trust in my heart for Your plan, even when I cannot see it. Strengthen my steps, calm my fears, and help me walk forward with reliance on You."* (Ch. 5)

*"Ya Allah, strengthen my faith and let my heart be firm in yaqeen. Help me trust Your love for me more than my fear of disappointment."* (Ch. 6)

## FOR PROTECTION OF INTEGRITY

*"Ya Allah, protect me from all forms of shirk, both obvious and subtle. Grant me the wisdom to recognize practices that compromise Tawheed."* (Ch. 3)

*"Ya Allah, protect my integrity. Let every step I take be rooted in obedience to You and guided by Your light."*(Ch. 10)

## FOR HEALING AND CLEARING BLOCKS

*"Ya Allah, remove the doubts and wounds that distance me from Your mercy. Heal my heart so I can receive from You fully."*(Ch. 11)
*"May Allah ease your pain, lighten your burdens, and make what is difficult easy."*(Ch. 11)

## FOR ASKING AND SUPPLICATION

*"Ya Allah, let me never hesitate to turn to You. Open my heart to ask You with clarity, sincerity, and trust."*(Ch. 5)
*"Ya Allah, if this is good for me, make it easy. If it's not, redirect me to what's better."*(Ch. 5)

## FOR ACTION AND GUIDANCE

*"Ya Allah, guide my steps and bless my efforts. Help me take action from a place of trust rather than fear."*(Ch. 7)
*"Ya Allah, if this step is good for me, give me courage. If it's not, redirect me to what's better."*(Ch. 7)

## FOR GRATITUDE

*"Ya Allah, make me among the grateful. Let my heart recognize Your gifts, both large and small."*(Ch. 9)

## FOR DAILY GUIDANCE

*"O Allah, I intend to walk in integrity, serve where I'm needed, and stay grounded in Your remembrance. Guide me, protect me, and open doors that are good for me."*(Ch. 12)

## FOR LIFE TRANSITIONS

*"Ya Allah, guide me to work that is halal, fulfilling, and allows me to support my family while growing in my deen."* (Ch. 14)

*"Ya Allah, guide me through every season of my life with wisdom and grace."* (Ch. 14)

## FOR COMMUNITY AND RELATIONSHIPS

*"Ya Allah, connect me with mentors who will guide me toward what pleases You, and make me a beneficial mentor to those You place in my path."* (Ch. 15)

*"Ya Allah, surround me with righteous companions who support my growth in both deen and dunya."* (Ch. 15)

## CLASSICAL DU'AS REFERENCED

Istikhara Du'a: *"Allahumma inni astakheeruka bi'ilmika, wa astaqdiruka bi qudratika, wa as'aluka min fadlika al-'azeem, fa innaka taqdiru wa la aqdir, wa ta'lamu wa la a'lam, wa anta 'allam al-ghuyoob. Allahumma in kunta ta'lamu anna hadha al-amra khayrun li fi deeni wa ma'ashi wa 'aqibati amri, faqdurhu li wa yassirhu li thumma barik li fihi. Wa in kunta ta'lamu anna hadha al-amra sharrun li fi deeni wa ma'ashi wa 'aqibati amri, fasrifhu 'anni wasrifni 'anhu, waqdur li al-khayr haythu kana thumma ardini bihi."* (O Allah, if this matter is good for me in my religion, my life, and my end, then decree it for me and make it easy for me, and bless it for me. And if it is bad for me, then turn it away from me and turn me away from it, and decree for me what is good wherever it may be, and make me content with it.) *Source: Sahih al-Bukhari* (Ch. 7, 14)

Morning Remembrance: *"Alhamdulillah al-ladhi ahyana ba'da ma amatana wa ilayhi al-nushur."* (All praise is to Allah who gave us life after having taken it from us, and unto Him is the resurrection.) (Ch. 12)

Tawakkul Declaration: *"Hasbunallahu wa ni'mal wakeel."* (Allah is sufficient for us, and He is the best disposer of affairs.) *Source: Qur'an 3:173* (Ch. 2)

## FINAL REFLECTION DU'A

*"Ya Allah, Let my heart remain close to You. Let my dreams be a reflection of trust, not attachment. Let my actions be rooted in sincerity. Let my striving be lightened by surrender. And let my life be an answered du'a—pleasing to You and aligned with Your wisdom. Ameen."* (Final Reflections)

# Additional Essential Du'as for Your Practice

## For Beginning Any Task

*"Bismillah al-Rahman al-Raheem"* (In the name of Allah, the Most Gracious, the Most Merciful)
Use: Before starting any endeavor or daily practice
*"Rabbish-hurni wa la tu'akhirni, wa yassir li amri wa la tu'assiruhu."* (My Lord, hasten for me and do not delay for me, and make my affair easy and do not make it difficult.)
Use: When seeking ease in matters

## For Sustenance and Provision

*"Allahumma akfini bi halalika 'an haramika, wa aghnini bi fadlika 'amman siwak."* (O Allah, suffice me with what You have allowed instead of what You have forbidden, and make me independent of all others besides You.)
Use: When seeking halal provision
*"Allahumma barik lana fima razaqtana wa qina 'adhab an-nar."* (O Allah, bless us in what You have provided for us and protect us from the punishment of the Fire.)
Use: Gratitude for blessings received

## For Forgiveness and Purification

*"Astaghfirullah al-'azeem al-ladhi la ilaha illa huwa al-hayy al-qayyum wa atubu ilayh."* (I seek forgiveness from Allah the Mighty, whom there is no god but He, the Living, the Eternal, and I repent to Him.)
Use: For comprehensive forgiveness

*"Rabbana atina fi'd-dunya hasanatan wa fi'l-akhirati hasanatan wa qina 'adhab an-nar."* (Our Lord, give us good in this world and good in the next world, and save us from the punishment of the Fire.)

Use: Comprehensive du'a for both worlds

## FOR STRENGTH AND PATIENCE

*"Rabbana afrigh 'alayna sabran wa thabbit aqdamana wansurna 'ala'l-qawm al-kafireen."* (Our Lord, pour upon us patience and plant firmly our feet and give us victory over the disbelieving people.)

Use: When facing challenges or opposition

*"Hasbiya Allah la ilaha illa huwa, 'alayhi tawakkaltu wa huwa rabb al-'arsh al-'azeem."* (Allah is sufficient for me; there is no god but He. In Him I trust, and He is the Lord of the mighty throne.)

Use: For complete reliance during difficulty

## FOR KNOWLEDGE AND WISDOM

*"Rabbi zidni 'ilman."* (My Lord, increase me in knowledge.)

Use: When seeking understanding or making decisions

*"Allahumma arini'l-haqqa haqqan warzuqni'ttiba'ah, wa arini'l-batila batilan warzuqni'jtinabah."* (O Allah, show me truth as truth and grant me the ability to follow it, and show me falsehood as falsehood and grant me the ability to avoid it.)

Use: For spiritual discernment

## FOR FAMILY AND RELATIONSHIPS

*"Rabbana hab lana min azwajina wa dhurriyyatina qurrata a'yunin waj'alna li'l-muttaqeena imaman."* (Our Lord, grant us from among our wives and offspring comfort to our eyes and make us an example for the righteous.)

Use: For blessed family relationships

## FOR PROTECTION

*"A'udhu bi kalimat Allah at-tammati min sharri ma khalaq."* (I seek refuge in the perfect words of Allah from the evil of what He has created.)
Use: General protection from harm

## FOR EVENING REFLECTION

*"Allahumma a'inni 'ala dhikrika wa shukrika wa husni 'ibadatik."* (O Allah, help me to remember You, thank You, and worship You in the best manner.)
Use: Evening gratitude and commitment

## FOR TIMES OF DISTRESS

*"La hawla wa la quwwata illa billah."* (There is no power and no strength except with Allah.)
Use: When feeling overwhelmed or powerless
*"Allahumma rahmataka arju, fala takilni ila nafsi tarfata 'aynin, wa aslih li deeni kullahu, la ilaha illa ant."* (O Allah, it is Your mercy that I hope for, so do not leave me in charge of my affairs even for a blink of an eye, and rectify for me all of my affairs. None has the right to be worshipped except You.)
Use: When feeling lost or in need of divine intervention

# ABOUT THE AUTHOR

Fatimah Linda Howard brings a rare and powerful blend of spiritual devotion, professional leadership, and lived transformation to the topic of Islamic manifestation. A passionate student of Islam, she has spent decades integrating meditation, mindfulness, and vision-based goal setting with a deeply God-centered approach—grounded not in trends, but in *du'a* (supplication), *tawakkul* (trust in Allah), gratitude, and purposeful action.

She is the architect of the seven-step Islamic manifestation framework presented in this book—one she has personally lived, refined, and now shares with you. Her commitment to visualization, vision boarding, and inner alignment has helped her build a life shaped by intentionality, divine trust, and meaning.

Though not a traditional Islamic scholar, Fatimah is a devoted seeker of knowledge who has traveled extensively in the Muslim world and written on Islamic family life, end-of-life care, grief, and ethics. Her first Islamic focused book, *Crescent Over Crossroads*, chronicled her journey as an African American Muslim woman navigating identity, purpose, and faith—establishing her voice in the growing field of Islamic personal development.

A sought-after speaker on Islamic spirituality and wellness, she has presented at respected venues including Yale University's Annual Shura & In-Service Training, the International Muslim Mental Health Conference in Jordan, and the Annual Muslim Mental Health Conference hosted by Michigan State University's Department of Psychiatry. She has also facilitated an educational session at Claremont School of Theology and regularly hosts Sisters' Steadfast Saturdays—a monthly gathering fostering connection, reflection, and sisterhood among Muslim women.

As a mentor, consultant, and leader, Fatimah has guided individuals and organizations through transformative change. With more than 35 years of professional experience in law, compliance and ethics, and diversity, equity, and inclusion—including senior roles such as Chief Compliance Officer and Associate Vice President of Business Ethics—she brings both spiritual depth and strategic clarity to her work.

In *From Vision to Divine Provision*, she invites you into the sacred process that has shaped her life—and offers a spiritually grounded, practical path for aligning your dreams with divine direction.

# CONTINUE THE JOURNEY WITH FATIMAH LINDA HOWARD

If this book resonated with you, imagine what's possible when we go deeper—together.

Fatimah Linda Howard offers a range of services to help individuals, organizations, and communities align purpose with divine wisdom:

KEYNOTE SPEAKING Inspire your audience with presentations on Islamic manifestation, ethical leadership, and authentic success. Perfect for conferences, corporate events, and faith-based gatherings.

1:1 COACHING Transform your leadership approach through one-on-one coaching that integrates spiritual principles with professional excellence. Find faith-based clarity, confidence, and transformation.

RETREAT FACILITATION Guide groups through intensive manifestation workshops using the seven-step framework from this book. Ideal for organizations, Islamic centers, and personal development groups.

BOOK SIGNINGS & WORKSHOPS Bring the principles of *From Vision to Divine Provision* to your community through interactive workshops and meaningful book signing events. These sessions offer a chance to engage deeply with the seven-step sacred manifestation framework, grounded in Islamic values and lived experience.

Fatimah is also the author of *Crescent Over Crossroads*, a compelling spiritual memoir that chronicles her journey as an African American Muslim woman navigating identity, faith, and purpose. Book signings can include discussions from either book—or both—tailored to your audience's interests.

Whether you're hosting a masjid gathering, women's retreat, campus event, or interfaith space, Fatimah's sessions are designed to spark reflection, connection, and inspired action.

CUSTOM PROGRAMS Tailored programs for organizations seeking to integrate ethical practices, diversity initiatives, and values-based leadership.

**Connect with Fatimah:**

visit WithLindaHoward.com

or email connect@withlindahoward.com